Praise for *Approaching Enlightenment:*
A Guidebook for Buddhist Ritual

I can't think of anyone more on fire with the magic of ritual than Bodhidasa. Whether he's weaving playful, groundbreaking spells with kids in Buddhist schoolrooms or bringing something mysterious and life-changing to seekers online, he is, in the words of poet Elizabeth Bishop, 'a believer in total immersion'.

Bodhidasa's own devotion shows in this always surprising, wonderful book. It will lead anyone who's curious, sceptical, or passionate about ritual to a better understanding of what it's really all about – in heart and in mind. This book isn't just for Buddhists – it's for anyone who wants to recapture the magic of their childhood, or pull on the golden threads of story and connection that run through any life.

Bodhidasa's wise words give us the courage and strength to choose to practise with our whole selves, and see where that might take us in any moment, when we can sing free of whatever is holding us back. In this book, Enlightenment is right there as a beautiful presence, and it will make you glad. – **Candradasa**, author of *Buddhism for Teens* and founder of Free Buddhist Audio and The Buddhist Centre Online

Bodhidasa has given us a beautiful guide to understanding ritual, bringing in its magical and mysterious nature, as well as giving down-to-earth practical suggestions. He takes us in a refreshing and engaging way through Triratna's Sevenfold Puja. I recommend this book to anyone practising the Dharma, the experienced and convinced, as well as the more sceptical. Once I started, I couldn't put it down. – **Khemasiri**, co-founder of the Triratna Buddhist Centre in Amsterdam

In a world where the word 'ritual' is usually prefaced by 'meaningless', it's a joy to read this insightful and accessible exploration of the power of puja. Bodhidasa explains with clarity – for the sceptic as well as those drawn to puja – what Buddhist ritual is really about, and how puja can transform our minds and imbue our lives with meaning and significance.

So often, meditation is seen as 'the real deal', whereas the power of puja to transform our minds is seriously undervalued, even amongst long-standing Buddhist practitioners. Yet ritual can touch parts of our psyche that no other practice can reach. I hope Bodhidasa's book will invite many people to enter into their own creative explorations of puja and see for themselves the transformative effects. – **Maitrisiddhi**, Buddhist teacher, Taraloka Buddhist Retreat Centre

Do devotional practice and ritual have any place in the life of a modern Buddhist? Straight from the heart, and drawing on his own explorations within the Triratna Buddhist Community, Bodhidasa offers an overview of the territory and, above all, the challenge all Buddhists face: to find emotional equivalents for their intellectual understanding. – **Nagabodhi**, author of *Sangharakshita: The Boy, the Monk, the Man*

Bodhidasa succeeds in writing both for the newcomer to ritual as well as the old hand: responding to the questions we inevitably ask ourselves – but are sometimes afraid to ask aloud – and offering fresh insights in equal measure. With wit, intimate knowledge of the terrain, and a vivid imagination, he makes a compelling case for ritual as a path to Enlightenment. – **Prajnaketu**, author *of Cyberloka: A Buddhist Guide to Digital Life*

The Flemish poet Maeterlinck once observed, 'Poetry has no other purpose than to keep open the great roads that lead from the visible to the invisible.' We could say the same of the purpose of Buddhist ritual and the practice of puja. This rather neglected area of Buddhist practice is explored in accessible and practical language by Bodhidasa. For most of us, our Dharma practice is not about greater understanding, in some purely cognitive sense, but a willingness to connect with and refine those emotions that will enable a deeper engagement with the invisible mystery of reality. This book invites us into that deeper engagement, as Bodhidasa artfully moves us into a closer relationship with symbols, stages of puja, and devotional practice in general. The book is an intelligent person's guide to ritual and puja and will be of value to all those who wish to tread 'the great roads' that Maeterlinck spoke of. – **Purna**, preceptor within the Triratna Buddhist Order's ordination process in New Zealand and Australia

Bodhidasa invites us to awaken our imaginations and to see the world as a magician might in this delightfully unpretentious book. He skilfully shows us how, far from being extraneous to the Buddhist path, ritual lies at its heart – because it lies at the heart of human life itself. – **Subhadramati**, a member of the ordination team at Tiratanaloka Retreat Centre and author of *Not About Being Good*

Ritual is an essential part of the Buddhist path, helping us engage our emotions with the spiritual ideal and enter a deeper relationship with that ideal. And yet it's frequently misunderstood, undervalued, or even dismissed. In this book, Bodhidasa offers an accessible and progressive exploration, showing how engagement with Buddhist ritual can benefit not just ourselves but all beings everywhere. – **Vajrashura**, teacher in the Triratna Buddhist Community

APPROACHING ENLIGHTENMENT

A Guidebook for Buddhist Ritual

BODHIDASA

W

Windhorse Publications
38 Newmarket Road
Cambridge
CB5 8DT
info@windhorsepublications.com
windhorsepublications.com

Cover design: Katarzyna Manecka.
Cover image: Painting of Avalokitesvara by Aloka, 1974/75.

Typesetting and layout: Tarajyoti

British Library Cataloguing in Publication Data:

A catalogue record for this book is available from the British Library.

ISBN Paperback 978-1-915342-35-5

Contents

About the Author

Bodhidasa is a member of the Triratna Buddhist Order. He leads retreats, classes, and courses at the Sydney Buddhist Centre emphasizing the role of devotion in the spiritual life.

Bodhidasa studied English literature, history, and performance studies at the University of Sydney. He gained a master's degree in teaching, and has taught in some of Sydney's most prestigious schools on both sides of the city's beautiful harbour. Bodhidasa has been recognized as a leader in learning design and education, being twice nominated for the Australian National Excellence in Teaching Award and receiving a coveted international Churchill Fellowship in 2010 to explore programmes that support compassionate connections for young people in online spaces.

In his professional career, he is part of the leadership team at Australia's only Buddhist school, which caters for primary and high school students. Here he leads in curriculum design, play-based learning, and chaplaincy in addition to delivering classroom teaching.

His book *Approaching Enlightenment: A Guidebook for Buddhist Ritual* adapts and expands upon a course devoted to exploring the way rituals such as the Sevenfold Puja can support spiritual development and lead to powerful insights.

Bodhidasa lives with his partner and fellow Order member Manichitta in the Inner West of Sydney. Here they share their love of the Dharma, film, pop culture, and music with their incredibly old goldfish Ammy (short for Amrita – the Deathless).

Author's Acknowledgements

I wrote this guidebook so that it would be of value to those who wish to connect more fully to the practice of Buddhist ritual, regardless of the tradition in which readers practise. There have been many significant individuals who have helped shape my understanding and practice of puja.

My mother Jean Caldwell first opened the world of words to me when I was three years old. Through the *A Book of Children's Names* and the works of Dr Seuss, I learned to read and came to relish the power of words. My mother learned in the final weeks of her life that this book was to be published. She was proud of the achievement, and, despite little interest in Buddhism, promised 'to read every word'. Perhaps in her next life she will do just that...

My private preceptor Ratnavyuha remains a stalwart support to all my endeavours. He has always encouraged me to 'search for the magic' wherever I find myself. He believes, as I do, that we can find that magic in our own tradition so long as there are those who maintain the search.

My public preceptor Nagabodhi has influenced this book by instilling in me a need for devotion to be more than just a yearning to escape from pain. What is the point of flying in the sky if we lose the ability to walk on the ground?

I am grateful to my Order brother Prajnaketu, who passionately encouraged me to pursue teaching about devotion. You can hear a talk I gave to the Oxford sangha called 'Breaking the chains' here: http://bit.ly/Bodhidasa_BreakingTheChains. This talk encapsulates the ideas contained in this book in their earliest form.

To Dhiramati (who does not know me) I give deep thanks. In 2007 I attended a Buddhafield festival in Devon whilst dealing with a great amount of anger and grief. His leading of a Padmasambhava puja broke through the blockages and helped me heal. I learned the power of puja that day. You can find his own excellent pujas here: bit.ly/Dhiramati_Puja.

To my partner Manichitta, who also revels in puja: it has been a delight to share them with him. His stalwart presence and encouragement always lift me from the dark places.

I am immensely grateful to Khemadhamma, who led the first Sevenfold Puja I ever attended in 2000. It was just him and me in the shrine room. I giggled like an idiot through the Avalokitesvara mantra as it brought back images of watching *Doctor Who* in the 1970s: I was reminded of a Jon Pertwee story called *Planet of the Spiders*, in which the mantra is used to summon giant talking spiders from outer space. Despite this ridiculous recollection, the door to a whole new world was opened, and I am thankful for that.

I am indebted to the thoughtful and encouraging feedback provided by Dharmachari Purna in one of the earliest drafts. Other encouragement came from those marvellous people who joined the 'Breaking the chains' courses and retreats over the past five years (the content of which has informed this book): I am moved by the insights you gained. In particular, I want to rejoice in Callista Bryan, Alex Piggott, Mel Bell, and Nic Toscan, who have become dear friends and been helpful in ways they may never have imagined. You are each Dharma heroes!

To Dhammamegha and Dhatvisvari at Windhorse, I bow. Your insights and capacity to spot purple prose and passive voice at 50 yards is unparalleled. Whatever is clearly and crisply expressed in this book is their doing. Thank you!

Lastly and mostly, I thank Bhante Urgyen Sangharakshita. In 2005, I asked him what I should do when faced with competing demands:

'The Order members tell me to study this, meditate this way, don't do that, give up this... what should I actually do, Bhante?'

'Rest your heart on what brings the most joy', he said.

'That's puja', I noted, suddenly aware of the truth in the words I had just uttered.

'Hmmm. Then practise puja', he concluded with his fingers steepled.

And that's what I do.

Publisher's Acknowledgements

We would like to thank the individuals who donated through our 'Sponsor-a-book' campaign. You can find out more about it at https://www.windhorsepublications.com/sponsor-a-book/.

Windhorse Publications wish to gratefully acknowledge a grant from the Future Dharma Fund and the Triratna European Chairs' Assembly Fund towards the production of this book.

For Kate Orman who walks a different path,
but set me up on mine
and
For Manichitta who was the reason
I stepped onto the path in the first place.

I don't know where prayers go,
or what they do.
Do cats pray, while they sleep
half-asleep in the sun?
Does the opossum pray as it
crosses the street?
The sunflowers? The old black oak
growing older every year?
I know I can walk through the world,
along the shore or under the trees,
With my mind filled with things
of little importance, in full
Self-attendance. A condition I can't really
call being alive.
Is prayer a gift, or a petition,
or does it matter?

Mary Oliver, 'I happened to be standing', from *A Thousand Mornings*, Charlotte Sheedy Literary Agency

Prologue

Callista's Story

I first met Callista at the Sydney Buddhist Centre. She was an ethereal presence at Saturday morning meditation class, where she might stay for a cup of tea before evaporating back into the foot traffic. In the shrine room, I would see Callista's steadiness in meditation. Her expression evoked the luminosity of a Renaissance painting – pale and framed by a halo of gold-grey hair.

I got to talking with Callista. It turned out that she wondered about the need to remove shoes in the shrine room, though out of politeness she did take hers off. But it struck her that old wooden flooring was often very cold. Her busy mind and the temperature distracted her in meditation, which was her main reason for attending the Buddhist Centre. Was removing shoes completely necessary?

Her introduction to mindfulness was through an external pain management course. Soon afterwards, she located her nearest meditation centre, a place recommended by the instructor with the contented demeanor whom she so admired. What Callista encountered when she walked through the door, however, was confusing. Yes, there was meditation, but there was a lot of other stuff going on. 'There was a lot of bowing and chanting', she recalled, and 'what appeared to be religious iconography' on the walls. Callista saw these as eccentricities that had nothing to do with what she was there for, and that were not connected to what she understood meditation to be. And they certainly did not accord with her world view. They seemed like some form of magic that made her feel 'a little uneasy'. Yet something kept igniting her curiosity. Perhaps it was her training in scientific enquiry that drove her to keep asking, at least to herself: what was it with all the bells, smells, and multicoloured men sitting on flowers?

So, because she was too self-conscious to ask and no one volunteered explanations, Callista decided she would not bow, or chant. These actions were clearly for those of a religious inclination, and she did not even remotely have one of those. Callista's training informed her that, if something was not supported by corroborating evidence or at least some logical reasons, it was best respectfully put to one side. Callista was never outwardly critical or dismissive of these practices, but she was mildly troubled by the fact that no one felt the need to explain these ritualized acts in a way that made sense. Was ritual a taboo subject, or was this knowledge only for the initiated?

Of course, people did eventually try to explain the 'ritualistic elements' to Callista. They talked about rituals, and about something called puja and about archetypes; they talked about 'moods' (lots about evoking seven specific moods), but this only further mystified the rituals rather than shone light on them. Callista did not want to know 'about' rituals – she wanted to know how to get 'into' them, to get inside them and see what would happen.

And then Callista's innate curiosity got the better of her and she decided to attend a Buddhist devotional practice. It did not go well. She described the proceedings as 'over the top' and incredibly time-consuming. She had questions, but did not want to cause offence by asking them because the event seemed to be of great significance to those who were attending. She observed that many in the shrine room seemed elated or profoundly moved, whereas she left feeling bewildered and profoundly tired. Perhaps it was something lacking in herself, she thought. Was there a part of her that was not trained to appreciate this kind of magic? Perhaps her sharp analytical mind was not tuned into the wavelength of devotion? She wondered, with a sense of loss, if the power of Buddhist ritual practice would always be denied her.

But, ever curious, Callista began to stay for more than the meditation and ethically sourced tea. She stayed for Dharma talks and discussion circles, though mostly as a silent observer. Silent, yes, but keen-eyed.

Time passed as it always does. Callista tentatively made connections with others, and then deep friendships started to emerge at the Buddhist Centre. She continued to be silent when others were saluting the shrine, chanting, or prostrating. Then a course – not on meditation, but on ritual – was offered. Without a moment's hesitation, Callista signed up, hoping that this would finally be the opportunity to ask her questions and have them answered in a way she could appreciate.

This book has its genesis in that course.

This book outlines one way of approaching Enlightenment, and coming into relationship with that profound awakening and freedom. Unlike a lot of Buddhist writing on mindfulness, kindness, ethics, or the study of ancient texts and teachings, this book turns to this neglected but powerful and effective area of Buddhist practice – ritual.

The ritual that will receive the greatest focus is the 'seven-limbed practice', which was brought into and adapted within the Triratna Buddhist Order as the Sevenfold Puja. My sources are the core devotional texts and practices from the Triratna Buddhist Community, supplemented with teachings from Urgyen Sangharakshita and his longtime friend Lama Anagarika Govinda. Govinda's *Foundations of Tibetan Mysticism* and Sangharakshita's *Ritual and Devotion in Buddhism: An Introduction* are essential reading (we will return to these later). Other material comes from seminars and works by Sangharakshita's own teachers as well as more recent research on the power of ritual.

This guidebook is intended to bring understanding and perspective to ritual, rather than give you encyclopedic details. Stop when you need to stop. Practise and reflect where you find it necessary. There is no need to race through to the end and miss the sights. Sangharakshita once noted that too much reading and academia can actually hurt your practice,[1] so it's best to reflect upon and apply what actually works to give greater meaning.

I'm writing from the context of the Triratna sangha and its ritual practices. And I am also confident that there is something of value here if you practise in another Buddhist tradition. This is especially true for those who encounter activities that seem to hold great significance at temples, Buddhist centres, or gompas, but where the meaning is not made explicit. If you are curious to know some of the potential of these practices, then read on.

Rituals are symbolic acts, and, as we will see, symbols contain complex meanings that are fully unlocked through repetition and reflection. Whether you feel averse to ritual, are cautiously curious, or surprise yourself by absolutely loving it, this book provides a map of the territory. But also remember, at regular intervals, to put the map aside and open your eyes to take in the view.

Having done the course on ritual, Callista now understands why there are candles; she can explain why there are bowls on the shrine and what everyday practice they offer us. She now realizes the power of walking barefoot towards the Buddha statue. She can tell you that the words we chant together point us in the direction of a path beyond the limitations we experience in life. She knows the answers to some of her questions, and now has greater courage to ask even more challenging ones.

Callista's well-trained mind has not diminished. Rather it has been applied to an area of Buddhist practice that can open her heart and draw out her deepest longings and motivation. Callista knows in herself that she is not deficient, and never was. And, with respect for her own abilities, she knows that her analytical mind was not an impediment to understanding ritual – it was the means. She has learned what lies beneath and inside the words and the actions of puja. She has learned how to bring them into her life and let them work their magic.

Will you?

Chapter One

Is Buddhism a Form of Magic?

Buddhists today, especially those from outside the old Buddhist world, have embarked on a long and difficult journey to discover the image of the Buddha within themselves and to allow that image a natural expression in their own cultures. This work is more akin to magic than to science.

Subhuti, 'Reimagining the Buddha'[2]

1. So, what is magic?

Some of what Buddhists engage in looks a lot like magic. Depending on the tradition, there can be an occult air to the way in which bells, books, and candles are arranged on a shrine. Does the painstaking placement of coloured sand a few grains at a time into a memorized pattern or the weaving of a red thread around a wrist constitute magic? Add thick incense and fine wrought-metal instruments, and you may wonder if you have stumbled into a shaman's yurt rather than a Buddhist centre or temple. This must surely be just magic with different set dressing?

Magic is itself a complex word, layered with meaning; it can be used to describe everything from the quality of an experience to a form of entertainment, from a system of power to a source of evil and even to religion itself. Let's unpack this further.

Magic can be an unexpected moment, when an experience arises as if from nowhere and evokes a sense of pure wonder and awe – a miraculous sunset with the heavens on fire is magic. A rare bird landing on your shoulder and allowing itself to be fed. In those moments, the order of the world is rearranged, silenced, and new vistas are opened to you. Magic is a profound experience of wonder.

Magic is also a connection between people, such as the way a special someone looks at you or does something for you without asking. A gift arrives on your desk, dispelling your negative mood. A handwritten card expressing gratitude and appreciation for your efforts. This beautiful moment brings you ease, joy, or deep contentment. It seems to appear out of nowhere – as if, well, by magic. Here magic is a quality of profound human connection.

But magic is also the umbrella term associated with sawing a person in half and then miraculously restoring them to wholeness, or producing a rabbit from fancy headwear. This is stage magic or conjuring, filled with complex and ingenious trickery, where the audience is convinced of something that appears to have happened but did not. This is magic as an elaborate, entertaining, and often expensive deception.

And then there is the magic you find in Harry Potter, where waving a stick and saying something approximating Latin sends out beams of green light. This is the magic of fantasy fiction, and works in the realm of metaphor or allegory. Here, monsters stalk the moors and can only be slain by weapons forged with ancient spells. Here cantankerous wizards remind us to consider what to do with the rest of our lives. Here magic is a method to help us see our own mundane world in new ways. This is magic as allegory.

So, in the same vein, lighting incense, chanting mysterious syllables, and asking invisible beings to protect you from suffering could be seen as magic. Unfortunately, magic has gained a bad name due to unscrupulous magicians, who misuse their talents to manipulate others for profit. This is especially true of fraudulent spiritualist magicians who employ conjuring techniques to prey on others by summoning 'spirits' of the dearly departed. Then there are the showman magicians with their multi-million-dollar stage routines, who charge a premium for a night's entertainment. The legacy of these charlatans and stage magicians reduces magic to being an entertainment or worse. Magic in the truest sense of the word is not concerned with these shenanigans.

According to Chris Gosden, professor of European archeology at Oxford, engaging in magic has long been an important aspect of human culture. He sees magic as the 'continuity between the human will or actions and the world around us'.[3] It is a means by which we find our place in the universe and the universe in our place. For Gosden, magic exists alongside science and religion in what he calls a 'triple helix': each is an expression of curiosity that looks for structure, meaning, and awe in the phenomenal universe. Magic is the way for humanity to explore the seen and the unseen worlds – though it would be fair to say that this definition is also true for each component of the 'triple helix'.

Both science and religion search for answers; nowadays we see these as separate fields, but, according to the archeological record, magic was their parent. Consider how early alchemy gave rise to chemistry, astrology to astronomy and you have the idea. Since the dawn of humanity, magic has watched the sibling rivalry between religion and science with interest.

There are curious parallels within our own lives that mimic this historical progression from magic to religion and then to science. The paradigm or framework of magic is how, as children, we first make sense of the world. Think of the curiosity and imagination of young children who create causal connections where none may be present, and you have a sense of what I mean. Young inquisitive minds seek to find explanations for what they are experiencing. For example, a child may explain why it is raining by saying the clouds/God/angels/skies are crying, so we should try and make them/him/it happy if we want the rain to stop. They generalize, from their own experience of crying, that happiness stops the fall of tears. Think also of how children draw faces on the sun, trees, and clouds in their artwork. For children, the world is no more or less alive than they are. They see themselves in the world and the world in themselves. This seems little different from Gosden's definition of magic.

Furthermore, as adults we become co-conspirators in this magical view of the universe when we explain that a special fairy will pay cash for discarded human teeth, or that a 'jolly old elf' travels the world in a night delivering gifts to the good and coal for the naughty. Or, more poignantly, that Spot the ageing pet has gone to sleep and is now in a special place where all good dogs go, but you cannot ever see him again.

Our early forays into magic are not just explanations for how or why things happen. When we are read to or begin to read independently, myths and stories set in realms where magic happens teach us valuable life lessons and morals. When magic is evoked in these stories, it is almost always a synonym for personal agency and deep knowledge – the very things we may lack at a young age. In these adventures, magic is the hidden mechanism that makes the story world function. It creates the fiends that threaten the world, and empowers the heroes who act to save it. Only the skilled and capable have access to this secret world of magic. These are the wizards and seers and sorcerers.

Depending on personal circumstances, our childhood may segue from the magical to more religious or scientific explanations of our place in the universe. Schooling can attempt to present both frameworks simultaneously in awkward ways. Monday to Friday, we are introduced to the rigours of scientific method at school, and then, for those with a Christian cultural background at least, on Sunday we are invited to contemplate the mysteries of the divine. These two modes of posing questions and providing answers can be difficult for young minds to navigate.

A creative or destructive tension can persist through the teen years and beyond, as we seek to integrate two seemingly impossible models. For some, disempowered by more dogmatic religious rhetoric or disheartened by the mechanics of scientific empiricism, there is no returning to the innocence of a magical view. Gone are the faces drawn on clouds, because we now know the water cycle and we have long dispensed with the tooth fairy. But some individuals readily escape the conflict between the sibling paradigms to embrace magic. I was one of them. That is why I renounced religion, abandoned science, and instead became a ritual magician long before I became a Buddhist. Only then, once I had pursued the Buddhist path, did I understand the true potential of magic.

2. Magic and me

As a child, I looked on wizards in tales as role models because they not only had the secret knowledge of how the world worked, but they had the power to wield it and make change.

My first exposure to this came in a curious book of rhymes based on the alphabet called *A Book of Children's Names* by Janet and Anne Grahame Johnstone, published in 1969, a year after I was born. This book was on high rotation with Dr Seuss at bedtime. This was my introduction to the alphabet. Each letter was for the name of a different child, and a brief rhyme followed, outlining what each most enjoyed doing or wanted to become. It was always O for Oliver that I would spend the most time contemplating:

> Oliver in his overall
> is mixing a spell.
> He wants to be a wizard
> and he's doing very well.
> Lots and lots of magic books,
> inks in blue and green.
> He's trying to turn his woolly owl
> into a fairy queen.[4]

This was the birth of my interest in magic, spirituality, and personal growth. I wanted to be able to change things, change my circumstances and the personal difficulties I faced even at a young age. Oliver, with his mystical inks, tomes, and pet familiar seemed powerful. I've kept the book to this day as a reminder. (I also still have an orange woolly owl who remains steadfastly an owl despite my early efforts at transfiguration.)

As I grew older, characters such as Gandalf from J.R.R. Tolkien's works fascinated me by their odd placement in society – they were different from the majority, had strange mannerisms, were sometimes shunned, or belittled, but were unexpectedly significant. They were outsiders with a noble purpose. Moreover, they had an ability to set events in motion. These were characters like the White Rabbit and the Caterpillar from *Alice's Adventures in Wonderland*, Morpheus from the Matrix, and Yoda in the Star Wars franchise. (Later I saw similarity between these figures and the Buddha, Milarepa, Ryokan, and others.) I certainly didn't have any capacity to create their degree of change lying on my crocheted bedspread absorbed in books. Not yet anyway.

The most sophisticated exploration of magic I encountered was in Ursula K. Le Guin's masterful *Earthsea* series. Here we meet the novice wizard Sparrowhawk (whose true name, Ged, is revealed to him by his teacher). Sparrowhawk begins his life as a prideful boy, whose ill-considered actions bring calamity to the world. Le Guin charts his story from callow youth to disenchanted adult and beyond in a manner that cannot fail to leave an impression. Magic in these books emphasizes not the waving of wands, the casting of spells, and the making of potions, but a training in penetrating reality deeply – to know with a profound sense of intimacy the true name and nature of all phenomena, which is more akin to Gosden's view (and the Buddha's, coincidentally). Le Guin describes magic as a training in seeing:

> In that moment Ged understood the singing of the bird,
> and the language of the water falling in the basin of the
> fountain, and the shape of the clouds, and the beginning
> and end of the wind that stirred the leaves; it seemed to
> him that he himself was a word spoken by the sunlight.[5]

Inspired by these grand sorcerers, I pursued magic in its newest guise – that of modern paganism. I dabbled in druidry and divination, and eventually practised full-blown ceremonial magic for sixteen years, albeit mostly in isolation from other practitioners. Great tales from Norse poetry and the Icelandic Eddas fuelled my fatalistic romance of the past where the world seemed far simpler, more easily understood, and also more easily changed to fit my will through the weaving of spells. For the disaffected teenager and alienated young adult that I was, magic was a means to feel powerful in a world in which I felt powerless. According to the tradition in which I practised, there were forces at work in the world for good or for ill, and, if I were to placate them, serve them, admire them, then I too would share their power. Do the external work, and the internal would surely follow, wouldn't it?

If you find reading that paragraph somewhat troubling, it was also deeply troubling to live those years. Despite the promises, I found no power in ritual magic and certainly nothing in my training that enabled me to meet, let alone process, internal struggles. These years were marked with the opposite of what I was hoping to feel – I experienced a deep discontent masked by ambition and hefty pretension. Whereas others around me appeared comfortable accessorizing magic with all the best occult paraphernalia, I wanted more than my practice to be a hobby or a lifestyle choice. Despite this, something always held me back from crossing a line that, once crossed, makes it incredibly hard to return.

There is more to say on this aspect of my biography, and you will read of the moment when I turned away from this path and towards Buddhism in a later chapter. Suffice to say that, for me at least, magic was a way of avoiding taking responsibility for my own mind and the complexities that resided there. By focusing on external rites of sorcery, I was avoiding working on the actual internal source of my discontent. I found a truer 'magic', if you will, in Buddhism than I ever found in the pagan arts. Of course, this is not a condemnation of magical traditions, as everyone's contexts are different and many find great comfort and insight in the magical traditions, but it was not the medicine I required. That medicine was a hefty dose of Dharma, with an additional prescription of therapy. Religion and science re-entered my life.

Entering adulthood and the mental challenges it entailed, I, like many of my generation, found the need to face these trials with the support of guides. These were not the wizards of story, or my pagan elders, but they were nonetheless learned specialists in unique fields. They were therapists, psychiatrists, and counsellors who attempted to quell inner demons and help me confront spirits of my past. As for Sparrowhawk in *A Wizard of Earthsea*, my own thoughtless acts had wrought calamity perhaps not on the world, but on my mental health. Here, Gosden's third 'helix' reasserted itself – the strand of science.

As an offshoot of the scientific method, the therapeutic arts are cousins to the magical arts. Both require active investigation and imagination. To engage in either, you need to imagine a life that is different from the one you are living and then invest in a course of action that leads in the direction of the goal you envisaged. The limitations of therapy became apparent to me when, after many years of both psychiatry and psychology, I came to understand that the goal of both was to mend what appeared to be broken, and give it a good polish so that it seemed good as new. But just becoming better – more healthy, more whole – did not address the fundamental change for which I yearned.

Therapy employed rhetoric like that of the magic I found in novels and in the occult. All emphasized transformation, insight, and integration. In therapy I was asked to go within, encounter memories, harness my energies, and face forgotten traumas – just like Beowulf coming face to face with Grendel's mother, Gandalf with the Balrog, or Sparrowhawk with the Shadow. For that is the work of the true wielder of magic: facing up to what is present before you no matter how terrifying or how painful it might appear. But, however helpful it may be, therapy has its limitations: therapy might help you have the courage to look and to understand, but Buddhism teaches you how to see, to serve, and to let go.

3. The magician and the Buddha

The common factor in therapy, spiritual practice, alchemy, and magic is the transformation of one state or thing into another through a specific process or intervention. Whether this is a card or coin pulled from the ear as we find in stage magic, a ring of power that corrupts those who hold it, or a potion used to make someone appear as another, magic is at its heart concerned with metamorphosis. But it is the magician who enacts this change by applying consistency, wisdom, and effort. There is much we learn from and apply to Buddhist practice from the standpoint of the magician.

The origin of the English word 'magic' is key to understanding the true purpose and relevance of magic. According to the *Oxford Dictionary*, the fourteenth-century French word *magie* refers to 'shaping or influencing events' by using 'hidden natural forces'. Thus, a practitioner of magic is one who is able to uncover what is obscured, and then wield this knowledge to shape the events of the day. Magic or *magie* in this sense is not external to the world – it is not angelic, infernal, or something altogether alien. It is encoded in reality itself.

Magie has its ancestor in the Ancient Greek word *magos*, which is akin to the modern word 'mage' or 'magician'. *Magos* refers to one of the 'learned class' who has mastery of specific, hard-won knowledge or understanding. These are people who use their knowledge derived from exploration and investigation to create. It is from *magos* and its plural *magi* that common English words like 'image', 'imagine', 'imagination', and 'imagery' are derived. To imagine, to create an image, is to apply your hard-won wisdom, to create something real and affect or influence the world. Magic is not something wild and accidental – it is a skill to be honed and a craft to be mastered.

Further back still, the earliest root we have for the word 'magic' is the Old Persian word *magush*, meaning 'to be able'. Thus, magic is an ability, a skill, a capacity to enact and make. Magic is the act of a creator who brings things into being by accessing hidden forces. A magician is one who has honed those skills to perfection, and created something from the application of those skills. They then share this insight or power with others through a system of training.

That sounds remarkably like the Buddha to me. He was a well-trained man who directed his skills and abilities towards finding the cause of and a remedy for suffering. Initially he trained as a member of the warrior elite, mastering archery and the handling of other weapons. He would have learned about looking for targets and deciphering strategic strengths and weaknesses. In addition, he was also trained to lead and inspire, as he was primed to be a future leader of his people. These skills prepared him well for the alternative route he took, for they developed in him a keen eye, determination, strength of character, and empathy. Once he had attained his goal of Enlightenment, these unique insights were then communicated. He trained others in how to attain liberation.

In many ways, the Buddha was a magician. There are numerous accounts from the earliest scriptures of him engaging in actions that we might consider magical or miraculous. He frequently conversed with gods and monsters. He appeared to move faster than someone running to catch him, despite not even breaking a sweat. The Buddha is also recorded as rising into the air and releasing both fire and water in great streams. And these are but a few of the early records. Later texts, such as the vast array of Mahayana sutras, take these miraculous acts to whole new cosmic levels of the unexpected.

While not disregarding these stories as flights of fiction or poetic allegory, it is prudent to focus on what these tales do to illustrate the core aspects of the magician. They are concerned with individuals moving beyond limitations, perceiving different levels of reality that we are unable to access. Moreover, in these and other stories, the Buddha is a figure who acts solely to penetrate the very causes of suffering with the express purpose of alleviating it. Along the way, there were many dead ends and failures; the final result, however, was not only the complete transformation of an individual but the foundations of a new way of perceiving and being in the world. A process of change was outlined and communicated.

I am not the first person to describe the Buddha as a magician. The Buddhist poet and philosopher Asvaghosa, as far back as the early second century CE, wrote a text called the *Buddhacarita* or *Acts of the Buddha*. This epic poem contains a vast collection of epithets ascribed to the Buddha, each one capturing aspects of his character and the ways others viewed him. The list is exhaustive, and you would be hard-pressed, if you consider yourself a Buddhist, to not find at least one title or name that has some personal resonance. Here is a brief section with the terms related to the Buddha as magician highlighted in bold:

> The **dispeller of the darkness of ignorance**, Illuminator of the Great Torch; Great Physician, **Great Seer** – the Healer of all evils who is the extractor of the barb of evil from all those wounded by evil.
>
> He is possessed of all distinctive marks and adorned with all signs. With his body and limbs in every way perfect, of

pure conduct and perfectly clear mind, **possessed of the ten powers**, having great fortitude, **learned in all learning** [...]

"**Lord of all wisdom**": **the wise**, the destroyer of the pride of all disputers, **the omniscient**, the Arhat, **Possessor of Perfect Knowledge**, the Great Buddha, Lord of Saints;

"The Victorious": triumphant over-thrower of the insolence and pride of the evil Mara, the Perfect Buddha, Sugata, the wise one who **fulfills the wishes of all beings**,

Ever cognizant of past acts, never speaking falsely, a mine of perfect excellence and of all good qualities; **destroyer of all evil ways and guide to all right ways**.[6]

The aspects of the Buddha marked in bold highlight his impact as a guide and teacher, a holder of knowledge who sees into the truth of things. Referring back to our etymology of the term 'magic', he is most certainly of a 'learned class' who is able to 'shape events' with mastery of 'hidden natural forces' – the forces here could be considered as all phenomena and experiences, which arise in dependence upon conditions.

Of course, were we to highlight a different set of titles, we would see the Buddha as a warrior, or rebel, or a monarch, but the relevance of seeing the Buddha as a magician is his capacity to develop insight and his ability to communicate this to others. There is something timeless and archetypal about the Buddha – a person who sought answers, found them, and then guided others to the same realization through a unique path.

The archetype of the magician referred to earlier was made much of by the twentieth-century psychologist Carl Jung. He proposed a series of archetypal figures that manifest in human cultures, mythologies, religions, relationships, and stories. These archetypes can be seen as cultural templates that appear in different guises across human experience. The magician is just one of many.

An archetype is not a thing or essence, but a collection of tendencies or ways of acting in the world that seem to be common across many human cultures – it's a pattern or template. Archetypes emerge in dependence on certain situations. Think of the heroes who arise to save a community when it is beset by trials. Think of the mentors who guide them to achieve their aim. These universal characters help shape human behaviour and, in turn, shape our collective stories. These stories then shape us in turn, as we dwell upon them, retell them, and adjust them for time and context. Our stories make us, and we then make the stories that continue to shape us – that is at the heart of the model of the archetypes. Stories create themselves through us. We create ourselves through enacting stories. Stories and humans are in a process of co-creation.

At its core, the archetype of the magician is associated with mystery, alchemy, and transformation. Yes, magicians are the custodians of knowledge, but the archetype points to the potential and possibility of all to attain that degree of understanding. Magicians are visionaries, creators of sacred spaces within and without. Possessed of intuition and curiosity, they seek out ways to understand reality.

An excellent depiction of the magician archetype comes to us from the Tarot. This may seem an odd direction to take at this juncture, given that the Tarot is mostly associated with fortune telling. Yet there is more to the Tarot cards than helping us divine what might happen, as we shall see. I am reminded of Sangharakshita's words in *The Bodhisattva Ideal*, where he writes of the need for us in the West to connect with a range of myths and symbols, not just those that have come to us from Indo-Tibetan or Southeast Asian cultures. He writes:

> How as Western Buddhists will we engage in the creation
> of myth? On the one hand we have the whole Buddhist
> tradition, together with the mythology of Western culture,
> to inspire us.[7]

The Tarot is a central artefact of Western magical culture, which has humble origins as an entertaining card game called Tarocchi in the mid-1400s. It was only in the 1500s that the playfulness of the Tarot shifted towards a more occult focus. The image depicted here comes from artist and illustrator Pamela Colman Smith, whose work graces the most commonly available Tarot deck. Originally published in 1910,

the deck known today as the Rider–Waite Tarot is the template for most other decks. The elements of Smith's illustration deftly suggest the qualities and practices of a magician. These qualities resonate with aspects of the Buddha's quest and maybe your own. Could you be an aspiring Buddhist magician?

4. The magician revealed

The Magician Tarot card is a Western symbol of psychic and spiritual integration. There are many aspects of the card that support this. Firstly, the figure depicted wears an inner white robe, symbolizing purity of purpose, innocence, and an untroubled mind. Over the white robe, the Magician wears a red cloak, which reminds us of the outer world of energy and passion – the phenomenal world of experience. The partially hidden white robe suggests there are inner insights that are only revealed through action. The Magician dresses to be in the world, but close to the heart there is something radiant and pure. White lilies and red roses surround the figure, reinforcing this message. The flowers remind us that the natural work in which we are engaged exposes us to beauty, delicacy, but also thorns: such is the nature of our imperfect world. Pleasures, even the subtle fragrance of the rose, have their price. And lilies, being a Western symbol of grief and loss, are pertinent as a reminder that death awaits us all. The Buddha frequently reminded his students of the impermanence of all phenomena.

The red and white clothing is symbolically connected to the very essence of the Bodhisattva ideal. A Bodhisattva is a being who sets their heart and mind on Enlightenment for all – they act in ways that support this vision, yet remain in the world to assist and guide others. They act in the world but are not of the world. The Buddha too possessed great inner realization and wisdom. He was an enlightened being, but he still walked the same dusty roads as everyone else.

Spiritual integration is further highlighted by the gesture of the Magician in the Tarot card. One hand is raised to the heavens, wielding a wand – itself a straight line connecting two points. The other hand points delicately at the earth. Whatever insight is received from above, from the transcendent space, or from the beyond needs to manifest here in the phenomenal world. The Magician is that bridge that makes the beyond visible. This reminds us again of Gosden's definition of magic – 'continuity between the human will or actions and the world around us'. The Buddha's life illustrates both the destination and the way to arrive there.

It is worth noting that the figure depicted on the card is young. The form of the body is also hard to pin down to any particular gender. The youthfulness implies innocence or freshness, which is further supported by the verdant green undergrowth and flowers. This youthfulness might seem contrary to classical images of magicians like Merlin, Gandalf, Obi-Wan Kenobi, Yoda, and Albus Dumbledore, whose age seems to magnify their wisdom – they have lived long so that they must have gathered much insight. The Magician in the Tarot is still seeking, not in possession of wisdom but constantly, energetically on the quest for it. You need energy and vigour to keep seeking the truth. The young and the young at heart have that energy. A practitioner must remain enthused and open, rather than become old, closed, and cynical.

It is a curious parallel that images of the Buddha rarely depict an old man. He is nearly always young, healthy: even the Buddha on his deathbed is not shown as an eighty-year-old man. Bodhisattva figures – beings that work for the benefit of others – in the Buddhist tradition are also depicted as young, in the prime of life. Usually, they are shown as being around sixteen years old, at the height of their vitality. There is a timelessness to the Buddha and Bodhisattvas that is reflected in this Tarot card – a young magus at work.

The wand is a conduit for an individual's capacity to act. In the Tarot card, the Magician brings what is transcendent (at the top of the card) into the phenomenal realm. The wand is reminiscent of the vajra, dorje, or diamond sceptre that is often used in Tibetan Buddhist rituals. Like Zeus or Indra wielding lightning, the skilled Buddhist ritualist is able to hold on to an intangible power manifesting in the form of a vajra. The vajra itself is also a symbol of integration – the two halves, the skilful and the unskilful in unity, transformed by awareness and compassion. As a Buddhist, you are working to skilfully apply a powerful tool – using the mind to see the mind.

The belt worn by the magician is another potent symbol for integration. It shows a snake eating its own tail. Called the ouroboros in Greek, it

> is an ancient symbol depicting a serpent or dragon eating its own tail. The ouroboros often symbolise self-reflexivity, introspection, or cyclicality, especially in the sense of something constantly re-creating itself, the eternal return, and other things such as the phoenix which operate in cycles that begin anew as soon as they end. (alchemy).[8]

Firstly, this points to the capacity of the magician and indeed Buddhists to repeatedly look within, to turn inwards and seek spiritual sustenance in so doing. Secondly, through this and other actions we are creating ourselves repeatedly. The realm of karmic

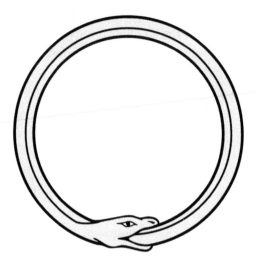

action is the working ground for magicians and Buddhists alike. This constant unfolding of directed and intentional growth is underscored by the infinity symbol hovering above the Magician's head, which has no beginning or end but cycles around without end. The magician is aware of the constant flux of time.

The Magician Tarot card is, in many ways, a template for the ideal Buddhist just as the Buddha image is. (We will explore the symbolism of traditional Buddha images in a later chapter.) Section 5 of this chapter will offer you a way in which you might approach not only this book and Buddhist rituals, but your whole Dharma practice with the qualities of the magician.

5. Something to try

We have thus far explored the etymology, history, and iconography of the magician in the hopes that the archetype may provide us with a positive start on this journey 'beyond' magic. Besides offering ideas and research, each chapter will also provide you with some techniques to try so that the book is less about theory and more about actual practice. This is intended to help integrate what you have read into an embodied reality.

As we have seen, this process takes patience and repeated effort. So I would urge you to revisit the following practices frequently as you move through the book, in order to keep your path as fresh and invigorated as the face of the young Magician on the Tarot card. The first practice is more of an attitudinal shift than a formal ritual.

#1 Be a magician

- Remain open-minded. Do not seek to hold on to ideas with fixedness and rigidity. Be open to what comes. The magician is not a fundamentalist, but a seeker.
- Make space for introspection, for meditation, for reflection, for silence and solitude, but also –
- Live, experience life, taste the world, and, with awareness of the consequences of your actions, work for the good of others.
- Act from your highest aspirations and values to the best of your ability. Keep doing that!
- Investigate and question what you see, feel, think, and touch with a kindly curiosity.
- Be present to the direct experience of the world, open to the elements in the ways they manifest, change, dissolve, and reform.
- Realize that you are a creator of yourself – you have agency and are not a pawn.
- Know that all you do and experience is subject to change. Each element of your life is borrowed for a time and then returned.

#2 Be a conjuror

Here's a little magic experiment. All you need for it is this book, an attitude informed by #1 above and a quiet place in which to work.

1. Feel the weight of the book or device you are reading this on.

2. Turn a page or swipe to the next. Then turn back to this page. The page moves back and forth due to your intent, effort, energy. Note the texture and temperature of the page or screen or keyboard as you do so. Try this a few times until you can discern different qualities of flow, texture, and warmth.

3. Feel the breath fill and empty from your lungs as you engage in step 2.

4. Move the book/device away from your hands where you can still see it. The book or device now occupies a different space, yet it appears unchanged. Or is it? Is it the same, or is it reduced in size in relation to you? What was there before you placed it there? What was there an hour ago? What might be there in a week?

5. Return to your memory of holding the book/device closer. Recollect the weight, texture, temperature, and breath taken while reading, and wonder where that recollection actually resides. Is it in the mind, the body, or both or neither? Is it in a place you decide is called the past?

6. Now, after a time, close your eyes and ask yourself – can the book/device be said to still exist if I cannot see it? Try this, then open your eyes. Of course it still exists, you say! You remember reading it, putting it down, opening your eyes to see it. But would the book exist if you did not have the capacity to hold it, perceive it, and recollect your sensory experience of it? Does the book exist without the mind that perceives it? Surely it does, you may think, because other people were involved in reading it, publishing it, editing it, writing it – but where are these people now in your experience? If they are in the past, how can they also exist now in your mind?

How is this book existing? What part do you play in its creation? Can you accept that your consciousness has collaborated in the creation of this whole process of the book, including the shop from which you bought it, the publishing company, the editor, and the author? You co-create, conjure up the entire arising of this book as if from nowhere.

So here is where we start the journey, with a magical premise. We begin with seeking an aptitude for awe. Buoyed by story, inspired by archetypes, and encouraged to investigate what we habitually think of as fixed or unchanging, we embody the magician's quest to know the truth. We are informed by Western cultural icons, which help us appreciate those from the East even more. But (and again it is a big but) what takes this further than magic is what we discover at the end of the journey and even perhaps in flashes along the way.

6. The chapter in review

We've drawn parallels between Buddhism and magic, going as far as to say that the Buddha was akin to a magician, and that the transformative power of Dharma practice is not unlike the mercurial forces of magic. Magic and Dharma practice have a lot in common.

- The origins of magic, religion, and science are in asking questions to find answers that provide a sense of satisfaction.
- Magic is not a derogatory and childish term.
- Even in early texts, the Buddha was referred to and described in language that frames him as a magician in the truest sense of the word.
- In the Triratna Buddhist Community, we are also reminded to look for the Buddha's universal truths within more familiar cultural frameworks.

- Western symbolism is adept at illustrating the qualities of a seeker of truth, freedom, and insight.
- The archetype of the magician contains helpful strategies and attitudes that can support Buddhist practice.
- Both magical traditions and the Buddha endorse the observation of direct experience.

Chapter Two

Buddhism Doesn't Have Rituals, Does It?

Food enchanted by a spell isn't fit for me to eat.
That's not the principle of those who see, brahmin.
The Buddhas reject things enchanted with spells.
Since there is such a principle, brahmin, that's how
they live.

The Buddha, *Sundarika-Bharadvaja Sutta*[9]

1. Busting the myth

If you have ever travelled in Asia, or even walked by a local Buddhist temple or meditation centre, you may have witnessed devotees engaged in ritual practices. I have been blessed with the opportunity to travel, and have observed incense offered in cauldron-like censers, precious gem chips poured into nested silver bowls, and sandalwood beads counted between nimble fingers. I have watched as people bowed to the ground in repurposed petrol stations and refurbished fire brigade buildings. The Buddhist Centre I attend has its main shrine room in a space that was once a printer business and, before that, the cool preparation room of a funeral home. So, regardless of the building, country, ethnic origin, and tradition, Buddhist rituals happen whether we are comfortable with them or not.

Buddhist rituals may have much in common with magic, but are they, well, Buddhist? The quote at the start of this chapter comes from a much larger story. of two people with different world views debating ritual practices. One seeks personal deliverance through adhering to tradition; the other is enlightened, and has a message for the ritual practitioner that is still relevant for us today.

In the story, a high-caste Indian or Brahmin named Bharadvaja is completing a ritual by the banks of a sacred river. The ritual is called a 'fire ritual' in the translation, which means the Brahmin was presenting a special sacrificial cake or piece of bread to a fire as an offering to one of the ancient Indian gods of the sun. From the remaining text, it seems clear that Bharadvaja was hoping the gods might intercede on his behalf and purify his past misdeeds. The gift of food would speed this purification process along, according to tradition. This transactional relationship is common in many ritual practices around the world.

After completing the ritual, Bharadvaja notices a man with a shaved head nearby and thinks, well, this man could be worthy of the burned-up remains of his offering, though only if he is also of Brahmin stock. Again, according to tradition, only one of such a status should be allowed to touch food offered to the gods.

The shaven-headed man is, of course, the Buddha, though Bharadvaja does not notice anything particularly out of the ordinary about him: no glowing aura, nor any other of the auspicious marks of an enlightened being.

The two men engage in a robust dialogue, in which the Buddha thwarts Bharadvaja's attempts at applying any classifications and labels to him. The Buddha denies being a Brahmin (a person of the highest caste) or descended from the merchant guild, or belonging to any other caste or category of persons. Bharadvaja almost takes his sacrificial cake away to offer someone else. Perhaps he wanted someone more grateful and less frustratingly honest to be the recipient of the gift?

The Buddha then makes a curious request of Bharadvaja. He asks the Brahmin to chant a prayer for him:

> Well, if you say that you're a brahmin,
> and that I am not,
> I shall question you on the Savitri Mantra,
> with its three lines and twenty-four syllables.

The Buddha was trained by spiritual teachers well versed in such prayers derived from the Upanishads. The chant to which Bharadvaja refers is a fascinating prayer to the sun that has survived to this day in several translations. Bharadvaja may know the prayer, but he is disinclined to oblige. He ignores the Buddha's request entirely, thus revealing much of his haughty character. A Brahmin is the one who asks the questions, not some shaven-headed ascetic! Instead of reciting the prayer, Bharadvaja asks the Buddha to explain why such practices as prayers and sacrifice even began. I imagine it as something of a, 'Oh, if you think you're so smart, why did these rituals to the gods even get started?'

Seeing the man's underlying concern for his own welfare beneath the question, the Buddha replies that, if he wants to find peace and seek his own benefit, he should attend to what the Buddha has to say. The Buddha starts to explain that rituals began in order to free one from past actions, but he is interrupted once again. Bharadvaja is quick to point out that this may be true, but, after completing external rituals of purification, it is hard to see the results. Do they work? Is one purified by making sacrificial offerings? Moreover, what ritual offerings are the most effective?

This is a good question. What do rituals such as chanting and offerings actually achieve? And by what metric or by what time frame can we measure their success? The question also reveals a flaw in Bharadvaja's spiritual practice that affects many: he does not understand why he performs these rituals, other than to maintain the tradition.

The Buddha then reveals what really needs to be offered up and sacrificed, and why a Buddha such as he is worthy of receiving such offerings. There is not space here to outline each of these offerings, but the key takeaway returns us to the quote at the opening of this chapter: awakened ones reject offerings that have been chanted over. In other words, you should not offer things up to receive something in return. Don't engage in a rite to establish or maintain a transactional relationship – offering a cake for special chants, blessings, and such. If you want to engage in an authentic and transformative ritual, just do it without expecting any form of reward.

Buddhist ritual practice, for the most part,[10] is not a form of sorcery in which you importune great spiritual forces in the universe, or bargain with them to provide you with power or grant you a wish. You are not at the mercy of such forces, nor trying to wrestle insight from them. To pray or chant or sacrifice to have spiritual forces intercede on your behalf has more to do with ancient systems of animistic practice than it does with Buddhism. For a ritual to be real and effective, the practitioner must know why they are doing it.

Here is another story that presents a curious twist on ritual. In this story, the Buddha encounters a young man called Sigala, who is going about his morning prayers. The man bows to the six directions as he was taught to do by his father, and he recites specific verses according to tradition. Curiously, the Buddha does not discourage the young man from his practice – rather he encourages the man to consider the deeper potential of it.[11]

After providing the youth Sigala with a lengthy exposition on the importance of living an ethical life, the Buddha repurposes the ritual of the six directions. When facing the east, recollect and offer respect to your parents. When oriented to the south, remember and offer gratitude to your teachers and mentors. Life partners and children are to be reflected on when facing the west. Respect and thankfulness can be offered to friends and colleagues in the northern direction. Those who support us with their service, those who work for us, are to be honoured by looking down, towards the nadir. At the zenith, above us, we express profound respect to those who are further along the spiritual path than ourselves.

In other words, to truly make offerings to the six directions, you must be thankful to all people in your life, those to whom you are intimately connected as well as those with whom you have a passing association. The Buddha does not condemn or dissuade the young man from actually doing the physical ritual of bowing to the six directions; rather, the man is asked to both see the practice in a new light and act in accordance with that view.

These are just two of many interactions where the Buddha asked people to question their motivations and clearly investigate the purposes of ritual. The Buddha was not anti-chanting or anti-ritual.

He was anti-ignorance. The Buddha acknowledged that for some individuals, such as Bharadvaja and Sigala, a path of ritual is a valid means of cultivating wholesome and positive mental states, but only if engaged in wholeheartedly and selflessly.

If the Buddha was not opposed to ritual, then why do so many of his contemporary followers struggle with it? The answer to this is simple but challenging. It reveals more about us than it does about the Buddha. The idea of the Buddha as a supporter of ritual is inconvenient for some practitioners because that version of the Enlightened One is not who they might want him to be.

2. The Buddha and the 'modern enlightenment'

Anyone encountering Buddhism has, at some time or another, to consider who the Buddha is for us today. As we saw in the previous chapter, there are people who consider that the Buddha was a great sage, a magician. Some may consider him a noble teacher who provided instruction and guidance on how to live a compassionate and ethical life. For others, Shakyamuni Buddha might have been a social revolutionary, who created profound cultural and spiritual change throughout Asia and beyond. What he offered us then can fix the wrongs of today. Others still may be inspired by his unwavering warrior-like commitment to following through on his quest to be free from suffering. And there are many who consider the Buddha to be a potent supernatural figure, or even something else entirely that cannot be so easily pigeonholed. Each understanding or way of drawing close to the Buddha is valid and a means of developing confidence in him as a positive force for change in our lives.

One of the more recent and popular avenues by which people approach the Buddha has been through developments in modern psychology, particularly the positive psychology movement. Mindfulness techniques offered by psychologists echo the Buddha's own teachings. The synergy between the old and the new is powerful. Given the frequent medical metaphors and the logical, inquisitive language of the early Buddhist texts, the Buddha can come across as a very early proponent of the scientific method.

This is not an unfair observation to make. Any reader of the early texts can see a highly empirical approach that asks individuals to examine a situation deeply, apply a strategy to amend or adjust the situation (in line with certain parameters) and then observe the response. The formulation of the four noble truths is just one of these rational, bilaterally structured teachings. And, what's more, the methods outlined by the Buddha do work, so it is fair to see the Buddha in this way – as an early pioneer of what we call science or even psychology.

For those of us who have trained in the sciences or in other analytical disciplines, it is comforting to see the Buddha as being in line with how we have been trained to see the world. Yet is that the sum of who the Buddha was? If he was a proto-scientist or a social engineer, how can we reconcile that with the way others revere him as a philosopher or a spiritual force? Who is correct?

Is our view of the Buddha, our response to the Buddha, dependent upon how he fits within our world view? Take some time to contemplate that. This is a controversial question, but one that has existed since the Buddha first walked the earth. Many who met with him wanted to know if he was a man or a god, or a brahmin in the case of Bharadvaja. The Buddha would reply that he didn't fit into any existing classification: he was a whole new form of being. Ask yourself a more nuanced version of this question: was the Buddha a highly developed human being who transcended the limitations of form, or was he a profound spiritual entity manifesting as a person? Which one of the two is easiest for you to accept?

Let's look at where the West first encountered this idea of the Buddha as a philosopher or early scientist. The interpretation of the Buddha as an exemplar of humanistic endeavour and as an embodiment of the modern age first emerged in the mid-eighteenth century. As proponents of the Western Enlightenment sought to free themselves from what many considered the oppressive and illogical elements in Christianity, the need for a leader remained. But this leader needed to be freed from unnecessary spirituality and ritual, for there was no room for such notions in an enlightened world. So, in casting out Jesus, they looked for another saviour to take his place.

Early European academics relished the opportunity to apply their freshly honed tools to new sources – in this case the Buddhist scriptures – and only saw what those tools enabled them to see. These scholars saw the Buddha in the texts they studied as the best version of themselves – rational, unemotional, reasoned, enlightened (in the historical sense), and, above all, scientific. After all, a vast number of written Buddhist texts contained logical expositions in regular, repeated formulas. So based on this alone, to scholars of the time, it followed that the Buddha was the progenitor of modern philosophy.

This is reminiscent of the axiom attributed to Anaïs Nin, but which has precursors in both Christian and Jewish texts: 'We do not see things as they are. We see things as we are.'[12] And so, elements of the Buddha's biography that were an uncomfortable fit for the scientific model, such as references to supernatural beings and rituals, were ignored. Colonial mindsets sought to elevate that which in Buddhism was more akin to the European view, and sought to excise that which seemed contrary to it. Ritual, for example, was labelled a later accretion, an artefact of primitivism and a corruption of the pure empirical teachings.

Donald S. Lopez is an esteemed professor of Buddhist and Tibetan studies at the University of Michigan who explores this in *The Scientific Buddha: His Short and Happy Life*. Lopez convincingly shows how the Western movement transformed the Buddha into

> a philosopher who rejected the rituals and myths of the
> Brahmin priests, a philosopher who set forth an ethical
> system, open to all, regardless of class and caste. A system
> based on reason. This transformation of the Buddha was
> made possible by the science of philology, the ability
> of Europeans to turn their gaze away from statues and
> towards texts, to look away from the Buddhists who stood
> before them across Asia, to look down at the Buddhist
> texts on their desks in Europe, and then imagine who the
> Buddha must have been. This was the moment when the
> Scientific Buddha was born.[13]

Standing as we do in the twenty-first century, we may look back at such a reductionist attitude with the benefit of hindsight. We know from experience, whether it be from exposure to meditation, personal Buddhist practice, or world travel, that the Buddha and indeed Buddhism cannot be condensed into something so limited as being purely a science, a philosophy, or magic. Yet it is always valuable to reflect on one's own views and see the ones to which we cling tightly. Again, I ask the question: how do you see the Buddha?

My own response to the Buddha has gone through several distinct phases. Early on, I treated Buddhism as a lifestyle choice, an accessory to my drab life, much as I had treated my practice of ceremonial magic. It was easy to pick and choose those bits that were a comfortable fit, like home furnishings, meditation props, mala beads, and Buddha statues that acted like spiritual air-fresheners. It was, in those days, much more convenient to buy a Buddha than to become one.

This materialist phase altered as my perception of the Buddha radically changed. Going on pilgrimage to places in India and Nepal that the Buddha had visited released a depth charge in my perception of the Buddha and of Buddhism. I grew ashamed of my rampant spiritual materialism. Standing in the dusty ruins and seeing the ardent faces chanting verses from the heart, I realized that the Buddha truly existed – he was not just some storybook character or noble idea – he was real. Buddhists themselves were not just members of a social group, a fandom, a club, followers of an aesthetic principle, or an association of people who were interested in talking about the Buddha. No, these were people who were deeply grateful for the opportunity to be free from the ties that bound them to suffering. Here I learned to see the Buddha as a liberator.

Being ordained into a Buddhist order – having that commitment to liberation witnessed and receiving the gift of my name – shapes how I see the Buddha. The name I was given serves both as a recognition of my devotion and as a path of practice. 'Bodhidasa' translates as 'He who is the servant of Enlightenment'. I serve and support others to encounter moments of awakening, and cherish the legacy of those who, like the Buddha, attained Enlightenment.

From day to day, I turn the jewel of the Buddha over in my mind, and different facets reflect both my need and his insight. That's the interesting thing about facets of a jewel: none can exist separate from the others connected to it. Each is a different shape but part of the whole. It is the way in which light moves through one facet to another, then through yet another, that makes a jewel shine – that is what makes it beautiful. So I choose not to limit my view of the Buddha or pin it down to one thing. To do so would be like trying to flatten a diamond with my naked thumb.

What I have come to learn, rather painfully as it turns out, is that, when we pick and choose what fits our world view, our way of seeing things, we affirm and adorn ourselves. We fix our identity. This is contrary to the core teaching of the Buddha, which states that we can know for ourselves that there is no fixed identity, and that, in clinging to one, we will experience suffering. If we examine the elements as outlined in the previous chapter, we will see for ourselves that nothing is owned forever – all is borrowed for a time, even our views. Holding on inevitably leads to experiencing pain. By holding on tightly to our own chains, we cannot be free. Just what these chains are, these bindings that keep us from freedom, will be the subject of Chapter 3.

Attitudes towards ritual can be informed by our understanding of who we think the Buddha was. If, as Lopez argues, we see the Buddha as an early scientist, we can only dismiss ritual. If we see the Buddha as a religious figure, then we may be more positively disposed towards ritual. Our views matter, and they can be changed. We will come back to this in Chapter 3, but it is more important now to get to grips not with who the Buddha was, but with what a ritual may actually be.

3. So, there are Buddhist rituals, but what actually *is* a ritual?

So far, I have purposely not defined ritual in order to allow your own thoughts to develop about the subject. From what we have explored so far, what do you think a ritual is?

We've explored some of the attitudes people have towards Buddhist rituals. They can be perceived as empty magic or as a distortion of the 'true teachings'. Rituals can be viewed as accessible only to the specially initiated, or as some form of religious theatre. It comes as no surprise that rituals are a major subject of ethnographic study at universities. Thankfully, many contemporary academics are more respectful and open-minded than their forebears.

Dimitris Xygalatas, an associate professor in anthropology and psychological sciences at the University of Connecticut, is one such academic. He has made it his mission to explore the power of ritual. His recent book on the subject is an enthralling read that argues the pivotal role of ritual in our own lives. It is not a book 'about' ritual: it delves deeply into ritual and its relevance to us today. Xygalatas takes us into the world and experiences of ritual practitioners through recounting visits to remote communities, as well as describing contemporary laboratory experiments designed to test the parameters of ritual.[14]

His research has led to some surprising findings, particularly about the ways in which the human psyche perceives rituals. Essentially, if an act is ritualized – formalized into a particular pattern or sequence – it is more easily remembered, and so too what is coded into the act is more easily recalled. Not only is it more easily remembered, but it is also recalled with greater clarity than if the same actions were not arranged in such a sequence. Xygalatas cites numerous experiments involving everyday activities that are performed with or without additional actions (in other words, some are ritualized and others not), and the results are astonishing – those simple things performed with redundant actions are reported to have greater significance and lead to the greatest changes in the participants. The book is a must-read.

Rituals are, according to Xygalatas, repeated series of actions that are framed in a certain order, performed at specific times, sometimes in special places and with codified objects. Many of these actions do not seem to have any direct function, yet they generate certain effects. Whatever the actions – whether they are making hand gestures, repeating special words, splashing water, lighting candles – all are done for what Xygalatas calls a 'causally opaque' purpose. In other words, there is no obvious connection between cause (the action) and effect (the overall goal):

> By their very nature, rituals are causally opaque: there is
> no obvious causal connection between the specific actions

they involve and their purported end goal [...] This gap between behaviour, intention and outcome is why rituals often seem puzzling, pointless or even comical to outsiders. But while causal opacity may look like a bug, it is in fact essential to ritual's ability to create special and meaningful experiences.[15]

Take chanting, for example. Sitting with others while making the sounds *om mani padme hum* to a particular tune does not correlate with acting compassionately. Yet, frequently, such an experience of chanting evokes a peaceful or even a heart-warming feeling of compassion, as if one were in a situation where one was being called upon to care for another. The words and melody of the mantra do not have a mechanistic cause-and-effect relationship.

A more rational and logical way to evoke warm-hearted compassion might be to give support to someone who needs it – for example, someone who has fallen down or someone who needs us to actively listen to their struggles in life. However, this is more likely to occur unexpectedly, and is only experienced by the one needing help and those providing it. Such an act would certainly form a connection, but only for a relative few at irregular intervals, depending on the circumstances. Ritualized acts that generate compassion can occur whenever such rituals are conducted, creating a potentially meaningful experience for the participants again and again. Moreover, these rituals become the training for when real-world compassion is needed.

Xygalatas also argues that the 'meaningful experiences' created by rituals are what first changed our ancestors from living lives of self-interest to forging sustainable communities based on shared values. The archeological and historical records repeatedly offer evidence of rituals playing a substantial part in early societies. Rituals of birth, coming of age, marriage, and death united us then as now in common stories and shared values. So too do the rituals at sporting events, legal proceedings, and celebrity events. In times of crisis and change, individuals and communities also seek out repeated actions that bring meaning and comfort. Xygalatas wonders what new rituals are being created as a means of responding creatively to the recent global pandemic.

Urgyen Sangharakshita, in his book *Ritual and Devotion*, draws on an earlier writer, Erich Fromm, for his definition of ritual, though it does not stray far from Xygalatas' own. Fromm saw what he called rational ritual (as opposed to neurotic ritual) as a 'shared action, expressive of common strivings, rooted in shared values'.[16] Again, this emphasizes the collective nature of ritual practice and its value-based underpinnings. Rituals have an active component, and are based on a shared sense of direction or purpose. Moreover, when rituals are connected to larger contexts and stories – such as religious frameworks – there is a potential for the heart to be uplifted even more.

When writing about religion and its value, Fromm was interested in the way an individual or a society's character is shaped by the tenets of a faith. As noted above, rituals are repeated, shared enactments of values embedded in a specific contextual framework. But, for Fromm, this was not just a dry academic observation: he saw that there was devotion in such repeated acts, a yearning or profound expression of love. Rituals are concerned with what you love, what matters most to you. But it is not enough to perform the rites: the rites must inform your general conduct outside of the ritual itself. According to Fromm, 'we are what we are devoted to, and what we are devoted to is what motivates our conduct'.[17]

Consider commonly repeated actions that you engage in through these definitions. What behaviours do you engage in with others repeatedly that have a common trajectory or purpose? What values are supported and nourished in such actions? What are you devoted to, and how does this devotion shape your behaviour?

Let me share my own responses to these questions. Besides meditating with others and performing Buddhist rituals, I frequently play board games with friends. These friends are not members of a Buddhist community – in fact, many are Catholic, and one is a priest. We play a variety of strategy and role-playing games for hours at a time, at least once a month. If someone is absent for whatever reason, we do not play – the 'ritual' would not have the correct components if someone was away. Sometimes the games are about winning with high scores, even beating others through careful manipulations of chance, but it is curious to see that the real win is in the camaraderie

Approaching Enlightenment

and the spontaneous flow of interactions. When we play as a team, there is a real sense of shared responsibility and agency. We value the power of play, true, but we mostly value what each person brings to the experience, what uniqueness they offer. I am moved by some of my friends' gameplay and clever improvisations. I am in awe of the insightful ways they use their resources to help us collectively vanquish a foe. Playing games, at least for me, is a ritual of connection and appreciation. I leave the sessions feeling cared for, motivated, and with a sense that no struggle is insurmountable. Confidence and positivity enter my life when I play games.

4. Origins of Buddhist rituals

The Buddha was not opposed to rituals – rather, he was opposed to mindlessly reproducing them, going through the motions if you will. The Vedic rituals of his time were of value, but only if one imbued them with meaning. But what of actual Buddhist rituals, rather than repurposed ones from other traditions? Are there such things as uniquely Buddhist rituals?

There is an astonishingly large collection of Buddhist ritual texts, devotional prayers, visualization practices, and pujas that hold a treasure of insights. In fact, there are hundreds, if not thousands, of pujas one can easily find online. There are forms that are hundreds of years old, while others were written recently. Knowing that, it may be of interest to explore just where the forms and structures of pujas arose in Buddhist history.

The earliest repeated refrain of worship and respect comes from the earliest recorded Buddhist texts. Originally, the teachings of the Buddha survived only in an oral tradition, but this changed shortly before the dawn of the Common Era, when they were written down first in Pali and then later in Sanskrit. In these early texts are verses of worship that describe individuals bowing to the Buddha, making offerings of food and other resources, and then, once they have received a specific teaching, vowing to see him as their teacher and pledging to follow him. This became codified into the 'Going for refuge' verses that we will explore later in greater depth.

As stated above, puja is an act of worship where offerings are made, and verses recited. This is not, at first glance, all that different from the ritual cake offering performed by Bharadvaja, though the purpose is different. There are many rituals, chants, and repeated actions that can be performed to connect with higher spiritual qualities.

Within the Triratna Buddhist Community, we regularly perform the Sevenfold Puja, which was first collated and performed in the 1960s, though its source material is far more ancient. Most practitioners in the Triratna tradition would know that the Sevenfold Puja is based on a text by the great Indian pandit Shantideva, but it may come as a surprise to learn that he is not the originator of the form.

The Sevenfold Puja is, by its structure and underpinning, connected to a much larger corpus of ritual texts known as the seven-limbed prayers or the seven-branched practice. These are practised in most if not all schools of Tibetan Buddhism. The seven-branched practice has, as is plain from the name, seven components that assist the devotee in abandoning that which is holding them back and building up wholesome, skilful actions that strengthen their resolve.

The seven components or structures of the seven-limbed practice are:

1. Prostration: physical, verbal, and mental acknowledgement of the higher place of spiritual beings. This may involve a simple lowering of the head or placing the body as low as possible on the floor;
2. Offerings – both real and symbolic or imagined – are made by the devotee;
3. Confession: a declaration of ethical faults to both the community and spiritual forces;
4. Rejoicing in merit: an acknowledgement of positive ethical and mental states;
5. Imploring the Buddha to turn the wheel of the Dharma: asking for a specific teaching or instruction that might be beneficial;
6. Requesting the Buddhas not to cease their involvement in the world: a request that the teachings remain available in perpetuity;

Approaching Enlightenment

7. Dedication of merit for the benefit of others: a selfless relinquishing of all effort and all personal benefit to others.

The earliest source for the seven-limbed practice is a profoundly influential text composed in sections over a period from about 500 years after the Buddha's death to approximately the fourth century CE. Known as the *Avatamsaka Sutra*, which can be translated as the *Flower Ornament Scripture*, this text was and remains an incredibly influential text in Buddhist traditions worldwide. This sutra is a collection of discrete stories that inform the reader of the breadth of the Buddha's teachings whilst also doubling as a practice guide for attaining Enlightenment. Above all, it is richly mythological, and contains deep and potent symbolism.[18]

One chapter of this collection is frequently separated from the main text. It is known as the *Gandavyuha Sutra*, and nestled within this very popular text is a relatively short series of verses known as the 'King of prayers' or the 'Prayer of noble conduct'. Drilling down even further, we see that the first seven sections of this prayer are called the 'Seven preliminaries for purifying the mind'. This piece sets out the motivation to achieve Enlightenment for the benefit of all beings through purifying ourselves from self-interest.

It is in this prayer, from a chapter in a Mahayana sutra written several hundred years ago in India and China, that we find the seven stages of what we call the seven-limbed prayer and the structure of the Sevenfold Puja as outlined above.

The 'Seven preliminaries for purifying the mind' is a beautiful and uplifting text, woven through with high aspirations and unfamiliar terms. It is a poetic piece that employs several themes to lift the reciter/reader from self-obsession and towards seeing the wonder of others, particularly those who teach the Dharma. The prayer is purposefully elaborate and descriptive to enliven the senses and to invite self-reflection.[19]

This prayer becomes a template for other great Buddhist texts throughout the centuries. The structure and thoughts within it influenced the Indian teacher Shantideva, who delivered the *Guide to the Bodhisattva's Way of Life* (*Bodhicaryavatara*) in around 700 CE.

This seminal work remains one of the world's most sublime spiritual texts to this day.

But, there is still more to the tale! The seven preliminaries from the *Gandavyuha Sutra* also had a significant impact on the formulation of a later eleventh-century text by the great scholar Atisha. Entitled the *Bodhipathapradipam* (which in English translates as the *Lamp for the Path to Enlightenment*), the text lays out in clear terms what is needed to make spiritual progress regardless of your disposition as a practitioner. Atisha quotes extensively from the 'King of prayers' cited above, going so far as to use the whole prayer as a preface to his own book. Atisha returns to the primacy of the 'King of prayers', and by association devotional ritual itself, by commenting thus:

> For those excellent living beings,
> Who desire supreme enlightenment,
> I shall explain the perfect methods
> Taught by spiritual teachers.
>
> Facing paintings, statues and so forth
> Of the completely enlightened one,
> Reliquaries and the excellent teaching,
> Offer flowers, incense, – whatever you have.
>
> With the seven-part offering
> From The Prayer of Noble Conduct,
> With the thought never to turn back,
> Until you gain ultimate Enlightenment,
>
> And with strong faith in the Three Jewels,
> Kneeling with one knee on the ground
> And your hands pressed together,
> First of all take refuge three times.[20]

Atisha's text makes a strong argument for the need for a structured path of practice in order to make spiritual progress. This path, he writes, begins with worship. Worship here is seen as a means of orienting the mind, heart, and body towards one's spiritual ideals. Adding to the need to offer the 'Prayer of noble conduct', Atisha asserts that one must go for refuge by expressing one's faith in the

Three Jewels. It is perhaps for this very reason that Sangharakshita inserts the 'Going for refuge' verses into Triratna's *Sevenfold Puja*, altering the form, but staying true to the purpose. For those unfamiliar with the term, going for refuge will be the focus of Chapter 8.

Regardless of the form or length of the text, the structure consists of seven steps that lead one through a series of discrete reflections and practices. At its heart, puja is asking you an essential question: what matters most to you? Whatever that deep truth is, puja says, it must be adorned, treasured, and lived out so that it remains a vibrant presence and source of inspiration.

A noble aspiration indeed! But why do we fall short of this wholesome, altruistic endeavour? What holds us back not only from being the best version of ourselves but from Enlightenment itself?

In the next chapter we will look at the chains that hold us back and how ritual practices such as puja can shatter those bonds. But, before moving on, let's stop talking 'about' ritual and its history and move 'into' our own experience by considering what we have explored.

5. Something to try

Trying something once is of value, but the nature of a Buddhist life is summed up in the word 'practice'. As Buddhists, we practise our practices – we repeat what we have been taught, with a rational faith in its efficacy. Let's start with something small, but with potentially far-reaching consequences.

Put aside some time to reflect on an action you do and consider why you do it. What was its purpose when you first took it on? What part does it play in your life now? Does it still have the desired effect or not?

A personal example is that, when I wake in the morning, the first thing I do is make a strong cup of coffee and sit quietly drinking it. On the face of it, this is a relatively harmless act, caffeine and one teaspoon of coconut sugar aside, but it has become a rote activity that is unrelated to the actual state in which I find myself upon waking. My initial intentions for making coffee were to help me wake up and face the day, as I need to be up impossibly early to get to work. But, even on days when I feel alert and ready to go, I still make the coffee almost on autopilot. Why is this? This requires more investigation, perhaps during that very morning coffee.

When reflecting in this way, watch for a tendency to be overly critical and flagellate yourself for actions you believe are harmful. Conversely, you may find that such reflection builds a sense of pride in your achievements. Regardless of your tendency, keep investigating rather than deciding quickly upon the answers. There may be more going on than you expected. Sit with the questions with an open-hearted curiosity. You may be surprised what further questions and answers arise.

6. The chapter in review

Go back and check if the summaries that follow match your own understandings.

- The Buddha encouraged people he met to rethink and repurpose the rituals they practised.
- Buddhism is often seen by people in contemporary Western society as a rational way of life. This is in part due to eighteenth-century thinkers who in essence 'created' a new Buddha that was in line with the intellectual ideals of the time.
- This view of the Buddha as a 'scientist of the mind' ignores or deliberately excises references to the Buddha engaging with individuals about the true value and most effective practice of ritual.
- Rituals do not always seem to be connected causally to the effect they are trying to give rise to, yet they seem to work.

- It is valuable to reflect on what we do repeatedly and to consider if it still meets the original need. Has it become an empty habit?
- Rituals such as the seven-limbed prayer or puja have a long and noble pedigree. Over hundreds of years, a form developed, particularly in the Mahayana schools, which placed altruism at the heart of spiritual practice. Here is a table that lays out the developments of ritual.

	Text	Authors	Structures
25 BCE	First known written records of the Buddha's teachings are produced in the Pali language in Sri Lanka (Pali canon)	unknown	1. Prostration 2. Offerings 3. Praising 4. Going for refuge
First century CE	First Sanskrit records of the Buddha's teachings made in India (Sanskrit canon)	various	
Third–fourth century	The *Flower Ornament Scripture* is compiled, including the chapter containing the 'Seven preliminaries for purifying the mind'	various	1. Prostration 2. Offering 3. Confession 4. Rejoicing 5. Imploring 6. Requesting 7. Dedication
Eighth century	The *Guide to the Bodhisattva's Way of Life*	Shantideva	
Eleventh century	The *Lamp for the Path to Enlightenment*	Atisha	
Twelfth–nineteenth century	Proliferation of seven-limbed prayers written	Various	
Twentieth century	Sevenfold Puja (based on verses from Shantideva)	Sangharakshita	Going for refuge verses added to the structure of the seven-limbed prayer

Chapter Three

What Holds Us Back?

'You are fettered,' said Scrooge, trembling. 'Tell me why?'
    'I wear the chain I forged in life,' replied the Ghost. 'I
made it link by link, and yard by yard; I girded it on of
my own free will, and of my own free will I wore it. Is its
pattern strange to you?'

Charles Dickens, *A Christmas Carol*[21]

1. The chains

Old Marley's Ghost in *A Christmas Carol* gets straight to the heart of how
we become enslaved to suffering. The Buddha, over 2,000 years earlier
than Dickens, saw a number of states of mind that bind us to pain and
a sense of dissatisfaction. These states hold us back, limit our potential,
and mire us in stagnation. The Buddha spoke of these evocatively as
'fetters', 'bindings', or 'bonds' that block us from experiencing freedom.
He did not choose the word 'fetter' without good reason.

Consider the experience of being physically chained up for a
moment. Imagine the shame and sense of powerlessness. To be bound
is to have limited movement, a reduced capacity to make choices. It
is hard or even painful to move, to travel or even say what you want.
Chains can harm us if too tightly attached, or if we fight against them
strenuously. The metal can dig into our flesh, wound us, incapacitate
us. We can die from those wounds. You are at the whim of other
people; their power over you is all that matters. Resentment mingles
with the fear within us. This is a grim reflection.

The Buddha chose the image of fetters and chains for its immediate, visceral associations with servitude and pain. There is little more dehumanizing and tragic than the image of bodies chained together en masse. The Buddha saw that we are all in such a state, we are all prisoners. He also saw that there are ways to sever those bonds completely. Life may be permeated with suffering, but there is a path to freedom. Of that you can be assured.

Yet, for many of us, our chains are not physical but environmental or cultural. Our experience of life can be limited by shackles of varying degrees of weight. One's social class or caste can be a limiting factor; one can also experience reduced educational opportunities and minimal financial independence. Both affect one's capacity for agency. It is significantly harder for the poor to receive quality education and earn financial security than it is for those who have sufficient capital. Whether the wealthy wield that privilege and knowledge is, of course, up for debate. Regardless, the experience of inequity can be crippling.

On a psychological level, self-perception and self-esteem can also be confining, but so can the emotional boundaries imposed by inflated ego and conceit. Essentially, aspects of our individual character and external circumstances can reduce our options in life.

But these are not, according to the Buddha, the main shackles that tether us in place. Being born poor or rich was not an impediment to those who sought Enlightenment in the Buddha's day. The very concept of caste was dismissed by the Buddha as an invalid way of deciding the worth of an individual: it was irrelevant and must be transcended. External bonds – cultural bonds – were not the real source of imprisonment.

What are the strongest chains, which are the hardest to break? Views. Our views. We have already looked at how the way we see the Buddha shapes our response to ritual. If you dissolve the views, you sever the bonds that hold you back not only from appreciating the value of ritual, but also from real spiritual progress.

2. The three fetters

In the tradition, the first fetter is *self-identity* or a *fixed self-view*. This is the perception of ourselves as permanently being a certain way. Examples

Approaching Enlightenment

of this can be as varied as, 'I'm a Sagittarius, which means I'm always incredibly stubborn', or 'I'm an INFJ on the Myers–Briggs personality scale, which means I'm introverted and driven by judgements of myself and others.' Or even, 'I'm not into ritual. I'm a meditator.' If we hold a view of this kind, we experience feelings, thoughts, and perceptions as 'ours'. Labels and opinions and tendencies become perceived as rigid truths. They are 'things' owned by another thing called 'me'. Those views also affirm one's identity, the very 'me-ness' of me.

Moreover, we assume that, as we contemplate thoughts, memories, and feelings, we attach a certain realness and meaning to them. The more we think them, the more real they are. Just like a wheel that leaves furrows in the mud: a trail is dug deeper each time the wheel turns. Those ruts are what we see as the fixedness of our self-identity. We see tracks as us, and neglect the motion of the wheel. We start to construct a sense of ourselves as being a certain way, which can become inflexible. This is who I am and who I will always be, we say to ourselves. To be more poetic, self-identity is viewing the cresting wave as the entirety of the ocean. We will return to this in later chapters, as we delve into the purpose of ritual.

Sangharakshita, the founder of the Triratna Buddhist Order and Community, translates this first of the fetters into accessible and practical language. He calls this first binding *the fetter of habit*. We can be habituated to consider ourselves a person who is practical, rational, pragmatic, who has no place for symbol and ritual. Such things we might consider childish or unsophisticated, or even beneath us. Affirming that view digs the fetters in more deeply into our spiritual flesh, so to speak. Sangharakshita makes the point that this sense of our identity is a construction; by changing our actions, we can change ourselves:

> Breaking the fetter of habit means, essentially, getting out of the habit of being a particular kind of person. It is only a habit you have got into. You don't have to be the way you are. There is no necessity about it.[22]

Essentially, to break this fetter is to unravel the view that you are limited, that you are a certain way because certain memories, experiences, and conditions have formed you. That view limits and reduces you and your potential. This wrong view begs the wave on the ocean, which we take as the whole ocean, to remain the same and unmoving. The Buddha encourages us to go beyond seeing ourselves as the wave alone, and to realize that we are the very vastness of the ocean.

The second fetter is *uncertainty, indecision,* or *prevarication.* This is an unwillingness to commit or to apply oneself to a process wholeheartedly. You could also call this doubt. You might doubt in the possibility of Enlightenment being attained by anyone. You may have reservations about the efficacy of a tradition or a practice. Doubt, in the form of questioning, is healthy and encouraged, but not when it stops us from making any effort.

Moreover, this fetter can manifest as a kind of half-hearted going through the motions because you are never fully prepared to take a stand. You participate up to a point because maybe, just maybe, something better will come along that you can commit yourself to. To continue the ocean and wave metaphor, this fetter is the equivalent of a surfer standing on the shoreline waiting for the right wave, and never running into the water to ride even one.

Sangharakshita sees this fetter as *the fetter of superficiality.* This, he says, is about being divided and not fully behind what we say. We might bow to a shrine or turn up to a meditation session, but our reasons for participating are underdeveloped. Perhaps we accept the culture of the Buddhist centre, and just do something because everyone else does. We call Sangharakshita 'Bhante' (an honorific for one's spiritual teacher), but do so only because others do it, not because we recognize him as our teacher. We might bow in a perfunctory way to the shrine as it is the established norm, not because we are moved to offer respect.

To be bound up with the fetter of superficiality is to put on a show for others and even, in a sense, for oneself. To file away at this fetter, we could try the ritual practices out, but do so with honest curiosity and genuine energy. Another strategy would be to try and see the fruits for yourself when the time feels right and you are ready to commit.

Approaching Enlightenment

The third of these fetters or views takes going through the motions to the next level. This fetter is known as *grasping rites and rituals as ends in themselves*. This fetter requires considerable unpacking. To hold to a ritual as being an end in itself is to – if you excuse yet another metaphor – mistake the map for the journey. A map lays out potential hazards and scenic spots, but it is not the breathtaking mountaintop vista itself. A person who grabs at rituals as being important *in and of themselves* is one who is determined to turn up, recite the verses dutifully, make the offerings, and then go home safe in the knowledge that the work has been done and rewards will indubitably follow. Whether their mind was wandering to the football scores or in anticipation of the coffee and cake after the class is irrelevant – at least they did the practice! That's all that matters, isn't it?

This is *the fetter of vagueness*, because you are honestly unsure of the purpose or meaning of what you are doing – you just 'take your medicine' dutifully, as prescribed. There is no true investment in the practice. One might assume that its meaning is so complex and esoteric that to have that knowledge would be an impediment. Conversely, one might just endure such practices in order to belong, not in order to progress. Sangharakshita says:

> Breaking the fetter of vagueness means being willing to
> think clearly. It means giving time to thinking things out,
> having the determination to think things through.[23]

As for the metaphor of the surfer standing on the shoreline never catching the wave, vagueness manifests in them turning up not knowing the tides or the severity of the dangerous currents, and having no interest in the safe boundaries set by the flags. Moreover, they might have all the gear but no idea how to stand on a board. Or maybe they are even afraid of the water...

So, to break the fetter of vagueness you do have to know something about what the practice is for, what it aims at, and what the various aspects of being a Buddhist entail. In this context, it is about finding out what rituals, rites, and practices are about. Not in a general sense, but in a detailed one. Otherwise, you can remain woolly and uninformed, further lashing yourself to the fetter of vagueness.

In summary, the three fetters of *habit*, *superficiality*, and *vagueness* bind us to seeing things the way we always have. They stop us committing to a true process of change. We can say we want to change, that we are committed to being new, being different, being liberated, but sometimes this is just lip service. If we are honest with ourselves, what we really mean is that we want everything to stay the same but feel better about it.

Just like the circular shape of a shackle or a chain, this keeps us spiralling around and around in place. To break the chains we need to challenge our assumptions, commit, and find out the meaning behind what we are doing. To actually change, we have to do and understand things differently.

3. Views and rituals

There are many views about Buddhist ritual. We have already examined the erroneous view that there is no such thing as a truly Buddhist ritual. We have seen that rituals have a long history within the Buddhist tradition. But we have also seen that views accompany them. Our attitudes shape the degree to which we wish to engage with ritual. There are some views that need to be seen and named, so that we may learn from them and rise above them. Here are three examples we might learn from. You may see yourself in one or all of these:

1. *My past is always right.* You can be habitually disinclined to practise ritual based on views that you hold about it. Views are formed through experience and influenced by one's cultural context, so it may be that your previous encounters with ritual had no meaningful impact. Time spent listening in scripture classes or kneeling in churches may have seemed unproductive or irrelevant to you at the time. Perhaps you believe that what was true for you then will always be true for you, regardless of the situation. The fetter of habit screws tighter.

   But this is an opportunity! Begin to see that what has happened need no longer bind you as it once did. Change is possible. Look to examples in your own life to see how your opinions and attitudes have changed. This view invites you to open up to the power of impermanence. To engage creatively with this view, look for examples of how change manifests around you with that same sense of curiosity we evoked in Chapter 1.

2. *My path is the right one.* Another way of viewing rituals is to look down on those who willingly engage in them. One might judge those who engage willingly with ritual as lesser practitioners who have a 'herd mentality'. Similarly, if one sees ritual as primitive or for those of limited capacity (sometimes referred to uncharitably as 'devotional types' by the questionably named 'wisdom types', who see ritual as lacking intellectual or psychological rigour), one is again fixing reality to fit one's own parameters. Again, you are affirming a self that is comfortable and safe. Superficiality digs into the skin.

Ritual practice has the potential to be a wisdom practice as much as other practices, such as Dharma study or analytical meditations. To see ritual as for some and not for others – for the emotional types, for example – is another example of the fetter of superficiality digging itself into you. Buddhist rituals of the kind we are exploring here are not dependent on one's gender, temperament, physical vigour, or even intellectual capacity. To practise Buddhist rituals such as the seven-limbed prayer or puja is to work at softening the hold that such delineations have.

To learn from this view is to look with open curiosity at the practice of others and see its value. How have these practices, which you might not at first understand, served them well? A practice of appreciation is suggested by those who hold the view that their way is the only way. When appreciation is watered with attention and curiosity, it blossoms into joy for others.

3. *The path is an unfathomable mystery.* From another perspective, you could assume that rituals have some

mystical or esoteric function that, if engaged in, will lead to some epiphany or spiritual awakening – just 'trust in the process' and the 'veil to the beyond' will part. In this model, ideas and indeed thinking itself are seen as barriers to something perceived as more rarefied and spiritual – something called 'experience'. This view of the obscuring power of the intellect that blocks one from 'profound experience' is the very sort of vague and woolly thinking the Buddha's teaching asks us to eschew. Ephemeral experience, no matter how pleasant or mind-expanding, is not the aim of Buddhist practice – liberation is.

Indeed, having experiences can be seen by some as the purpose of ritual practice. Feeling joy and rapture, releasing tension, seeing visions can appear to be the goal. But such experiences are not the goal of Buddhist ritual, though they may be seen as the endgame in other spiritual traditions. Experience is useful in as much as it highlights the reality of the human situation. Experiences and indeed all phenomena arise in dependence upon certain conditions. If you have 'an experience', know that it arose due to certain circumstances. However, expecting that experience to arise again, or indeed actively grasping for it, only digs the chains in more deeply. Habitually grasping for 'the feels' only lashes you to suffering that little more tightly with the bonds of desire.

Though it can be true that words and an overly rational approach can impede a fully embodied Buddhist life, and that there can be a divide between 'knowing' and 'being', to remove any rational or even intellectual understanding of a ritual is to be half-hearted. But to see ritual as something mystical and magical that cannot rest in the confines of thought is to be vague and not embrace the potential ritual has to offer. The chains of vagueness rattle.

Holding this view is a clarion call to be wholehearted, wholly embodied. Bring all of yourself to bear on ritual practice, and see for yourself that it can offer freedom. If you don't, there could be a painful internal battle between aspects of yourself. A human being can only fully invest in ritual if they bring all of themselves to the ritual: the head, the heart, and the body must be engaged. Know the purpose, cultivate skilful emotional states, be present in the body, aware of subtle or gross changes, and you will reap rewards.

4. How to view our views

A healthy place to start is to acknowledge that you have views in the first place – maybe one of the three outlined above, maybe others. Be discerning of your reasons and motives, not critical and judgemental. Look with kindly eyes at how you see yourself, how you see Buddhism, how you perceive religion or personal development in general. Investigate your motivation for participating in any practice or action, and do so with an inner smile – after all, we are all unenlightened and trying to find our way. Lastly, ask yourself if you know anything about the purpose behind the activities you participate in at the Buddhist Centre or when you do any kind of practice on your own. Be prepared to not have it 'right'. Then again, have you enquired about the practices by asking questions, or were you afraid that you might come across as ignorant for asking what others must surely know the reason for?

Earlier, I shared my experience of the fetters and the views they generated as an example of the reflection process. I did not know it as a child, but I was tightly fettered and bound up. Despite those long endless summers riding my bike and climbing trees, the inner landscape was much less spacious and warm. Habit manifested in my life in the form of extremely poor self-esteem, with bouts of clinical depression. I was, in my view, crusted with vice and sin. Some of it was born of my own family, some from what I now know to be intergenerational trauma. Within my upbringing, I was left feeling disempowered, frequently lonely (I'm an only child), and somehow broken. This experience I believed was unchanging and fixed. I was cursed always to be like this (view 1: my past is always right). The majority of this stemmed from an oppressive family environment and the prevailing Australian culture in the 1980s that did not embrace diversity or even represent it. I did not belong, and was 'destined' to be sad and lonely for the rest of my life.

I have already written of my early forays into ritual magic, which I now know was a strategy to find power in what appeared a powerless situation. My encounter with Buddhist ritual was informed by my mindset and previous experience of ritual. Back then, Buddhism seemed a means by which I might scrape off the foul accretions my very existence brought about. To be wholly accurate, I was hoping that the Buddha would do that scouring for me. In a shallow and superficial way, I saw rituals as a way of 'summoning' the Buddha and other great figures of inspiration from wherever they existed so they might 'save' me. I imposed my psychological need for healing onto ritual, and would not be swayed from this view for a good many years. Here the third of the views listed above came into play alongside the first – I was so wretched that only the mystical, unknowable power of the Buddha could save me. I didn't know what I had to actually do to change the way I felt, never mind how to do it. And even then, despite this yearning, underneath I was firmly of the opinion that I did not deserve salvation. The inner 'poor me' voice grew stronger rather than weaker. I used to feel that the more I looked up at the Buddha, the further away I seemed to be.

I have a curious memory associated with this time. It was a warm spring morning, and I recollect attending a festival day at my local Buddhist Centre. There had been a Dharma talk by an Order member I respected, and I, not yet ordained, was inspired by the topic. During the Sevenfold Puja, I made my way up to make offerings during the mantra chanting. In an ecstatic mood, I felt moved to make full-body prostrations towards the shrine. Others around me were doing so as well, so it seemed appropriate, yet something was not quite right about my technique. Whereas others were progressing forward down the shrine room as they prostrated – one prostration then a step forward, another prostration then a step forward – I found myself moving backwards! The inner view was made real! Soon I was almost colliding with those waiting behind me to commence their devotions. This was involuntary, and I do not know exactly how it happened. I felt embarrassed at the time, but later understood what I was trying to tell myself – if you don't change the unhelpful view, the ritual will reinforce it.

It is hard to discern exactly when these views began to loosen. Rather than a single catalyst, there seemed to be a series of moments in which I saw how my internal monologue limited my perceptions of myself and of others. Meditation played a significant role to be sure: through sitting and watching, what appears to be eternal and true is seen as illusory. But I would say that it has been in turning again and again to objects of devotion that I have grown less dark and encumbered.

5. Something to try

How can you come to know your views and keep moving forward, rather than backwards? See your views as questions rather than truisms, verbs rather than nouns. Watch for internal statements like, 'This is weird' or 'This is not for me.' Or 'I don't get it.' Breathe into those thoughts. This is not a time to give up: keep looking, keep enquiring, but do so with kindly and compassionate eyes. You don't have to get this right, but rather be open to see what you are being asked to try.

Go and visit your local Buddhist centre or temple. It does not need to be a Triratna Buddhist centre for this to be effective – your decision to go and visit is what is important here. Regardless of what centre or temple you choose, it is advisable to call ahead to see when visitors are able to attend. Have courage to go and be open to what you encounter there.

Ask if you can sit for a time alone in the shrine room. Just be there – no need to meditate or to sit in any particular way. I imagine they will ask you to remove your shoes first (more on that later).

You may experience fear, nervousness, and discomfort. That's dukkha – what the Buddha called the first noble truth of unsatisfactoriness. This experience of oddness or disquiet is normal. Meet that with those same patient, kindly eyes. Watch the way your mind starts to target and label objects you see set out before you. Note that interpretations will swiftly follow, and may well coalesce into opinions and views. You may find yourself comparing objects you see with those from your memories of religious or spiritual places – 'Look, there are candles there too, and a statue like we had one of Jesus.' Watch the process calmly and patiently, without fixating on being right or clever or spiritual.

It might be that, after a time, the analytical mind that defines and searches for likes and dislikes begins to settle. You might start to see new features and connections in the space laid out before you. Let those observations arise and fall too, like the breath.

Maybe, after more time, that curious mind will grow quieter, and you might start to feel your way into the space in a new way. Rest in the growing stillness. Maybe, depending on the space, you will encounter its sacredness.

What would this be like if the hall was filled with people encountering what you are encountering now? Would their experience be similar to yours? Now that is an interesting thought.

6. The chapter in review

We have spent time in this chapter opening to what may be some new perspectives – fresh ways to look at yourself and how you might approach ritual.

- We are all bound up in some way or another – aspects of personal psychology, social conditioning, cultural norms, and unexpected pitfalls all affect how we experience life.

- Views are constructed and can, given time and effort, be deconstructed. Patience and kindness are also great assistants in unravelling views!
- It is valuable to reflect on the views we hold about ourselves and others. Moreover, what we see as the goal of this life is perhaps the most potent view we hold.
- Our habits don't just define us, they are in fact what makes us. Habits are like worn furrows that show that, at some time, a strategy was effective, so we keep applying it even if the circumstances have changed.
- Going through the motions – joining in without exploring our underlying reasons – feeds a sense of vagueness or woolliness, and even sometimes an inflated sense of the spiritual.
- Assuming that a ritual will, by virtue of being done, have an effect is limiting. Rituals are made more effective if one has a blend of reasoned understanding and open-minded curiosity.
- Experiencing discomfort when facing challenges – whether in your everyday life, or even in encountering ideas in this book – is not a sign of failure or weakness. Rather, discomfort is noble because it can (but doesn't always, it must be said) point in the direction of a view that could be refreshed.

Chapter Four

What Do You Need to Conduct Rituals?

'You want to work spells,' Ogion said presently, striding along. 'You've drawn too much water from that well. Wait. Manhood is patience. Mastery is nine times patience.

Ursula K. Le Guin, *A Wizard of Earthsea*[24]

1. A short list

After visiting a Buddhist centre or temple, it may be tempting to think that, to begin a practice of ritual, one needs esoteric equipment and a large, dedicated space. You may have seen many items arranged in specific ways, and thus think it necessary to purchase special artefacts. There can be a tendency when you visit such places to create a shopping list – refined Japanese incense to light before a Nepalese Buddha statue, or a blessed string of semi-precious stones to add significance and, dare I say, power to your rituals.

Other spiritual and religious traditions have specific ritual wares that promise access to esoteric knowledge and experiences when used appropriately. Whether it is sage smudge sticks, raven feathers, freshly ground juniper incense, Himalayan salt lamps, exotic talismans, or crystal singing bowls – you can be sure to find objects to ornament a spiritual practice. This is not to dismiss such items as mere ephemera or souvenirs, but it is easy to mistake the contemporary rituals of acquisition, consumerism, and collection for the real deal. This is particularly true for those of us in the affluent West. As mentioned before, it is easier to acquire a Buddha than to attain Buddhahood.

There is only one essential item required to engage fully in Buddhist ritual, and that is not a physical thing at all. And no, it is not faith or even a special initiation. Or a robe, or a kesa. There is only one thing you need.

2. The treachery of images

For a number of years, I worked in a public library. As a student of English literature at university, I felt this was an incredibly apposite job for me. I had ready access to an extensive collection of texts to broaden my tastes, vocabulary, and vicarious life experiences. It was a far more varied and interesting job than many think. It was profoundly satisfying seeing regular borrowers and chatting about their lives, but mostly it was quiet, and I found it a haven from what I experienced as the restless hunger of the outside world.

But inside the library was a different kind of busyness: the hushed silence held a cacophony of stories, realities, and needs. Bodice-ripping romances were a few shelves away from gripping espionage thrillers. Adventures set in derivative fantasy worlds leaned their spines against worthier antecedents. The readers themselves, driven by need or desire, came to access magazines they could not afford to buy, research local history, or quietly canoodle by the disused encyclopedias. Everyone came searching for a story, and at the same time everyone was living out a story.

Every library is the same in that way, and every book is similar in that each person comes to it with their own drives, intentions, and experience. For some readers, Jane Austen is the pinnacle of literary achievement, while for others her work is romance fiction with longer sentences. The words on the page placed there with such care by Austen are the same for both readers, but the readers themselves are different. Jane Austen is not only the best author in the world, she is also the worst depending on the person meeting the text. It is what you bring to the book that makes all the difference. The experience of reading – the immersion in the world, events, and characters – is co-created and unique for each individual.

This is also true when one rereads a text. Reading *Emma* at sixteen and then again at thirty-two are completely different experiences. The masterful observations of manners and relationships may strike the younger reader as insightful. At thirty-two, you may lack the patience. No one ever reads the same book twice.

The same is also true of words themselves. Every word contains layers of meaning generated through centuries of application, connotation, and misuse. A word's meaning shifts and changes. Consider words like 'terrific', 'awesome', and 'gay', and you can see how their meaning has shifted over time as contexts and attitudes have developed. Definitions are, ironically, not definitive.

We can even begin to think that the words *are* the thing or experience to which they refer. Take the word 'dog', for example. Presumably right now in your mind you have a clear or indistinct awareness of what a dog is – appearance, habits, food preferences, size, breed, memories of interactions with, attitude towards, and so on. But the dog I am picturing and sensing is unlikely to resemble the one you are. (Mine is an adorable West Highland terrier.) In fact, we can never experience the same series of associations. You were not bitten on the heel by a dachshund at the age of six, and are not consequently wary around small, yappy dogs. I bring my experience of 'dogness' to the word itself. And then we have other words for dog, such as the French *chien* and German *hund*, and any number of other words to name the complex tangle of behaviours and forms that is a dog. Which one is right? None? All?

This co-creation of stories and ideas became clearer to me once I stopped working in libraries. Having completed university with a degree in English literature, majoring in the Romantic poets, and semiotics,[25] I found myself in the unenviable position of not being able to read without analyzing texts into submission. Reading become a joyless task thanks to the tools I had learned.

Salvation came in the most unlikely of forms – comic books. Comic books brought back the joy of reading. Once I entered the world of comics and graphic novels, the boundary between artist/writer/creator and viewer/reader/audience shifted significantly. I mostly have one man to thank for that.

Scott McCloud created a phenomenal book called *Understanding Comics*, which explains in incredible depth how meaning is constructed through layout, panels, image, and text.[26] It turns out that reading comic books is far more complicated than it first appears. By complicated, I mean that there are a great number of processes occurring of which the casual reader might not be aware.

McCloud's expertly researched book delves into our earliest cultures and the potency of symbolic expression, as well as the most disposable forms of print media. From cuneiform to *kawaii*,[27] McCloud assimilates a series of key principles that apply to any media in which images and text co-depend. He examines Western and Eastern art forms, and effectively creates a shared grammar for how comics construct meanings. Added to this, McCloud is an award-winning comic-book writer and artist, so it seemed a natural choice for this analysis of comics to be an actual comic book.

Here is but one small slice of McCloud's insights into the relationship between author, reader, and text. In these boxes, you are Scott McCloud, teaching yourself about the way symbolic representations work. You are both the primary deliverer of the information and the audience of the message. It is a simultaneous co-creation of presenter and audience. The words in the speech bubbles are McCloud's, but your direct experience of them is as your own voice. And assuming for a moment that you did not read that section aloud, you did not actually hear anything: the hearing is taken for granted.

Putting René Magritte's[28] thought-provoking painting to one side for a moment, these ten panels also move you through time – perhaps only a few minutes – as the topic is explored. In the gutters (white spaces between the panels), the Scott character moves his body and his facial expressions. You don't see these changes happen, but somehow you understand that a movement and passing of time have occurred. You 'paint in' the movement so that the scene has a greater sense of reality. The static images become empowered with energy and life. Scott moves his hand from displaying Magritte's work up to his chin and you understand, though it never actually happens, that movement has occurred. The unseen is seen and made by you, based on your previous understanding of similar gestures. Lastly, no one actually speaks in bubbles. The words are yours: you speaking as him, to yourself, in your own head.

What has any of this got to do with Buddhist rituals, you may ask? It brings us back to the overall question about what is needed for Buddhist rituals: just what is the 'thing' you need? Well, it's you. You need you.

We co-create the meaning with the ritual and the objects. We are as active in empowering rituals and ritual objects as those who created them. We give them additional power, not the other way around. Thus, ritual requires us to be trained in how to leverage that co-creation more effectively.

This does not mean that a text or an object does not contain significance of its own. The careful addition of codified images in religious art, the delicate choice of words and the placement of ideas in literature, Austen's observation of manners are all deeply significant. The creator of such pieces puts great time and care into weaving meaning into the substrate of the work. But we can never experience the text or artwork or song as they did. We can never fully appreciate the process, the decisions, and the choices made in the creation of an artwork. Once meaning has been placed in a text

Approaching Enlightenment

or artwork by its creator, it is up to us to see that work through our own lived experience.

This is why Magritte reminds us in his painting that images are treacherous, in the sense that they are unreliable in and of themselves. Images, particularly symbols, are unreliable because the more potent of them do not communicate their meaning openly. They require the perceiver to be open-minded to the potential of the symbol, and to apply a process of wise interrogation in order to access their power. Investigate how the painting is indeed not a pipe, yet it also *is a pipe* in a strange kind of way. This points us towards a sense of symbolic 'pipeness' despite being a three-dimensional object rendered in two dimensions. Magritte's image of the not-pipe, McCloud's silent lecture, books being timeless classics and forgettable trash: all point to the truth that what is deeply significant, meaningful, and powerful depends to a great extent on what you bring to it.

To unlock images, symbols, and rituals, you must truly investigate the many layers of co-created meaning. To fully appreciate a text, read a comic book, make the most of art. To conduct a ritual, one must deeply contact the symbolic meaning that is embedded within. Moreover, if one wants to be transformed by it, one must unite with the truth that the symbol embodies. This is no easy feat! Thankfully the Buddhist tradition provides us with the tools we need to do just that.

3. How can we make sense of symbols?

It is important to explore an active process by which we can access the most profound meaning of a symbol and so deepen our understanding. In doing this, we have an opportunity to loosen the bonds of the three fetters.

As illustrated above, rituals are more akin to symbols than they are to signs. A sign is unambiguous and has a clear, direct meaning. Consider a stop sign or a parking-space sign for people with disabilities. The meaning is immediately clear. A symbol, by contrast, can suggest a variety of meanings depending on the creator's intent, one's own capacities, the degree of instruction, and one's depth of personal connection. Symbols are also multivalent: they can have more than one value.

Within some forms of Tibetan Buddhism, four levels of meaning are ascribed to practices, specific teachings, and ritual items. These four levels also reflect the historical developments of Buddhism quite closely. Whilst each level becomes more abstract, it does not follow that the previous level is superseded or put aside. All must be present in order for one to gain the greatest insight and wisdom from an object, symbol, or ritual. These four levels are ways of moving more deeply into the power of ritual and symbol.

These levels will form the basis of our investigation into how rituals break the chains of the three fetters and help us work with our views. We will apply them to several Buddhist symbols and rituals as we progress. Later in this chapter, we will employ these four levels to the most common of all Buddhist ritual items – an image of the Buddha himself.

Here is an overview of the four levels:

1. Word/outer meaning: this is the external appearance of a symbol or object, for instance a vajra – its shape, colour, size, and the materials from which it is constructed. This level also includes the context in which you might find the symbol, as well as a literal translation of a word into our own language: the seeing and the saying. Here we will take the term *experiencing* to indicate the sense of contact with the symbol or object as it appears to us. This first meeting with a ritual image or a practice can have a profound impact or be a matter-of-fact moment that sparks curiosity. Historically, this level reflects the approach of early Buddhism, which emphasizes ethical practices as a means to interact with the external world in order to reduce clinging.

2. General/inner meaning: this appears when we are able to visualize or internalize the object or word. Our initial curiosity regarding the object or practice becomes a fascination. At this level, we can see the syllable in our mind or recall the shape and structure of the ritual object. We also begin to put energy and time into finding

out more. For example, I might know that a vajra is a representation of a thunderbolt and is held by certain Buddhist figures. I start looking for books or websites to find out more. Or I begin asking questions of spiritual friends or teachers. This level is about one's process of *understanding* what the symbol is pointing at. Here we are beginning to take in and assimilate the symbol to some degree: the intellect is engaged, and potentially the heart as well. This level corresponds to the Mahayana movement, which encouraged all devotees to know the meaning of the Dharma and practices for themselves.

3. Hidden/secret meaning: this is an understanding of the symbolic or deeper meanings built into the space/object that can be reflected upon to gain insight. At this level, we engage in further personal reflection, or receive direct instruction from one who knows the meaning(s) of the symbol in question. Thinking about the symbol, turning it around in the mind, and allowing associations to develop are all part of this process. The label 'secret' may refer to the fact that only an individual can make this level of effort, and, short of telepathy, one can never know the lived experience of another's internal practice. Taking the vajra as an illustration again, we might come to see that there are connections with mandalas, and that its various components point to different spiritual practices. The object is both a weapon and a map. How is that possible? This is the question we are left to ponder. So this level of meaning gives us something to question and seek clarification about. *Applying* the symbol creates changes in perception and in how we live with that symbol as a part of our lives. Historically, this level of practice is reflected in the Vajrayana, with its use of mantra, sadhana, and tantric practices. Starting in India but popularized in Tibet, this level of practice is primarily concerned with internal transformation and integration of all energies towards Enlightenment.

4. Ultimate meaning: this is seeing the object or word as representative of a wider reality, as indicative of a universal possibility. The ultimate level is knowing and realizing for oneself the deepest truth that goes beyond the symbol itself. This is, in essence, the symbol released from its shape or form. This level goes beyond a mere intellectual understanding, as integration is gained through reflection on each of the previous levels. One's life and way of being in the world are changed by the symbol in profound ways: one is engaged in *realizing* the truth. Returning to the example of the vajra, at this level we act as vajra. We see the phenomenal world as vajra. Our speech takes on the energetic and spiritual qualities of the vajra. To all intents and purposes, we *are* the vajra. This cannot be learned from books, or taught on YouTube or in a podcast. This level is where the boundaries dissolve, where we move beyond the historical into the realm of the enlightened mind itself.[29]

It is important to note that these are not labels or categories of information, but ways of penetrating and becoming that which is coded within symbols and in rituals. They point to action.

These four levels can be applied to many aspects of the Buddhist path. For example, they can be useful in exploring how you see a Buddhist teacher or guru. A teacher is, progressively, a normal human being (outer/experiencing), a spiritual friend one may learn from and with whom one may discuss anything (inner/understanding), a someone who sets you on the right path by providing pertinent personalized instruction (secret/applying), and also a manifestation of the Buddha's compassionate activity within the human domain (ultimate/realizing). The levels allow us to encompass the apparent contradiction of human frailty and the transcendent that can be present in a teacher.

The levels can also be applied to one's degree of commitment to the Buddhist path. Sangharakshita explores this using the model of levels of going for refuge.[30] On the outer level, he asks: do you participate in Buddhist activities because you were born into a Buddhist community or culture? Or, for those of us who come to Buddhism as converts: do you join in because others are doing it? (The fetters can be heard

Approaching Enlightenment

tightening...) Are you a student and finding out for yourself what resonates? Here we are moving into the inner level, where we begin to understand what is happening around us. Our knowledge may be incomplete or even incorrect, but we are striving to make sense of the path and apply it. The true level of practice, the secret work, is when we are truly being changed by what we are doing. The practice has moved deeper into our consciousness, and our lives are more in tune with the words we espouse. At the ultimate level, we have abandoned all limiting factors and cast off the chains; we are far along on the path, perhaps even arriving at the summit itself.

4. Buddha image as symbol

Earlier we examined an image of the magician as a model for the qualities we might bring when approaching rituals. Let's apply the teaching on the four levels to a specific ritual item with which you are no doubt familiar – an image of the Buddha. You will have encountered any one of the thousands of designs on your visit to a Buddhist centre, temple, or garden centre. Each Buddha image contains variations on the theme of the Buddha; in some the figure is tall, seated on a lotus, or standing, or even lying down. In some the figure is richly adorned or plainly attired. In fact, the oldest known image of the Buddha presently in a collection does not even depict him in meditation; rather, he is standing surrounded by gods who are worshipping him.[31]

The image we will apply the four levels to is one that presently finds its home in the collection of the Metropolitan Museum of Art in New York. As you begin to *experience* the outer level, you may have a personal aesthetic response to the image. Of course, it is a sculpture represented in two dimensions, so that already limits the potential of the form, but there are still a number of interesting aspects to it that we can experience. It shows a human figure seated in a balanced, almost symmetrical posture. The hair is intricately carved, as are the folds of the light cloth the figure appears to wear. The slightly open eyes gaze towards the ground. The hands are lightly clasped in the lap. The lips are puckered in a gentle smile. Clearly, this is a figure seated in meditation, though the style of the depiction is more reminiscent of Ancient Greek sculpture than we might expect. The

face does not appear, at first glance, to represent an Indian man, yet the archeologists and historians who curated this piece claim that this is a depiction of the historical Buddha. By reading more about this work's context and uncovering the symbols embedded in the iconography, we will come to learn more.

To grasp a greater *understanding* of this image, we need to place it in its context and appreciate the historical significance. This is a piece from the Turfan region of northwestern China. It dates from between the third and fifth centuries CE, and was once placed inside a larger monument dedicated to the Buddha. This artwork belongs to the ancient Gandharan civilization that once flourished in part of present-day Pakistan and Afghanistan. We know from the archeological record that this civilization was involved in extensive trade as far east as China and as far west as Greece, hence the Hellenic style of the sculpting. The statue, which was in the ownership of private collectors for some time, now resides in one of the largest repositories of art in the Western world. It has travelled a long way from its first home, where it was part of a shrine or a devotional image in its own right. Now, when it is on display, it is viewed as an archeological relic and as a work of art to be preserved for future generations.

This work contains many iconographic elements common to other Buddha images. The hair is cut short, or at least pulled up high in a bun. Later images make this an elaborate feature. We know from the archeological record that Indian men of a certain status wore their hair long. The early texts inform us that, before he became enlightened, the man who became the Buddha was a high-ranking member of the warrior caste, and so it is likely he wore his hair long and accessorized with elaborate jewellery. The hair cut or tied up suggests that he relinquished his status as a high-born man. The earlobes, without heavy earrings, also point to this renunciation of wealth and power. The clothing in the image is also unadorned: the figure seems to be dressed in simple thin cloth. It clings to his form, but it remains light and almost diaphanous. What does this image imply about the nature of a Buddha as an enlightened person? Does it suggest anything about how we might best practise? This takes us into the secret realm of the four levels, where we begin to reflect and act on what the image is sharing with us. This image offers us a guide to being more like a Buddha ourselves. This statue is more than an object of devotion or veneration, it is a path of practice.

Consider the posture and alignment of this Buddha figure: straight back, body balanced and grounded. The figure is alert but steady. Let's apply this image as a personal reflection on our own spiritual path. This statue invites us to consider the way we conduct ourselves in the world. To *realize* Buddhahood, the statue implies that we must *apply* such steadfastness and uprightness in our day-to-day life. Can we sit still for any length of time? Are we constantly fidgeting and searching for stimulation, or are we able to calm and steady ourselves? Applying the image can go even further than this. Do we remain constant in our practice of truth seeking, or are we lurching from one new teaching to the next? Do we maintain our principles, or allow them to lapse due to forgetfulness or worse? If we can emulate this posture both externally and internally, our confidence will grow.

Symbols such as this Buddha image invite us to question how we live our lives and *apply* ourselves to practice. The hair and long earlobes empty of adornment invite us to consider to what extent have we renounced status and cultural expectations as we move along the path. Are we prepared to, as the historical Buddha did, put aside societal norms to pursue our quest for liberation? The half-open eyes suggest that one does not fully hide from the world, but remains aware of it. Eyes half-open and half-closed are a reminder for us to live in the liminal spaces between the outer world of form and the inner world of personal spiritual experience.

The delicate and almost translucent folds of the cloth also invite us to live simply and openly. The depiction of the simple cloth invites us to be less precious about discomfort and find bliss amid difficulty. Simple cloth in the summer. Simple cloth in the winter. Can we seek ease and consistency regardless of the circumstances in which we find ourselves? Also, in the subtlety of the clothing draped around this solid figure is the teaching that a Buddha embodies strength *and* vulnerability, vigour and gentleness at the same time. Lastly, the simple elegance of the cloth reminds us that there is a gossamer-thin veil between us and Buddhahood.

This sculpture is a relic of a time long gone and a culture long destroyed. It remains as a reminder that the quest for Enlightenment is one that transcends society, the borders of countries, ethnicities, and even time itself. Enlightenment is beyond such boundaries. The ethnic facial features of the figure, and indeed of any Buddha image, reflect the faces of the people in the society that produced it. Here they are the features of northern China depicted through the lens of Gandharan skill and aesthetics. In Kyoto the features are Japanese, Nepalese in Kathmandu, and broadly European at the London Buddhist Centre. This Buddha statue, and indeed all Buddha statues, challenges us to see that Enlightenment is not bound to one ethnic group or cultural expression: it is our human birthright regardless of our origins.

Placing a Buddha image in a place of significance such as a shrine or altar is to say to oneself and others, 'This is the path I follow; this is the goal I aspire towards, this is who I want to be.' Through continued reflection and practice, such an object becomes less of an ornament and more of a potent symbol for change. Eventually, through persistence, dedication, and deep seeing, you can *realize* the Buddha's own truth of Awakening and break free.

Now, these perspectives are my own based on the training and experiences I have gained. They are not absolutes or definite truths, but personal realizations and maybe even transpersonal ones, meaning that they might have some resonance with you. Remember Magritte and McCloud, who remind us that what we bring to any symbol co-creates the meaning.

In a later chapter, there will be instructions on how you can sit with images and allow yourself to see them more clearly and with greater depth. But for now, understand that even an image as commonplace as a Buddha is more than just a depiction of a person: it has the potential to illustrate a path to freedom.

5. Something to try

At the end of the last chapter, you were invited to visit a local Buddhist centre or temple. This chapter has explored the essential item or quality you need to access the many layers of meaning present in rituals and ritual items. Now, this your opportunity to find an image of the Buddha that you wish to connect with on a deeper level.

You may already be in the possession of a Buddha rupa (statue) or any number of other Buddhist figures. If so, this is an opportunity to apply the four levels to how you approach the image. If you are new to this, now is a good time to find a Buddha image, whether that is a statue or a picture. The form may be similar to the one discussed in this chapter or different. The hands may be arranged in the lap or in any number of other gestures. It does not matter which form you pick at this stage, as long as it is one that draws your curiosity and interest.

Once you have the image, take time to reflect on it by applying the four levels. Here is how you might do that:

1. Experiencing: what are the features of this figure? Take time to look closely at the face, hands, and posture. How do you feel when you sit with it? What thoughts and emotions arise?

2. Understanding: where did you find/purchase the Buddha image? How did you feel as you did so? Who made the image and what materials were used in its construction? What do you know about the Buddha's life and teaching? You might like to invest in a biography or an anthology of Buddhist teachings.[32] Consider opening up a dialogue with some Buddhists to hear what their response to the Buddha is. Talk with members of a Buddhist order to gain a sense of what the Buddha means to them.

3. Applying: after immersing yourself in the image and the life of the Buddha, extract some simple ways in which you could act that are in accord with what this image represents. This is an ongoing process, and not one that necessarily arises based on will. It may take a substantial amount of time to develop confidence in the Buddha as an exemplar, so there is no need to rush this. For example, you might be inspired by the Buddha's steadfastness and constancy, and decide to manifest that through being more equanimous with others.

4. Realizing: as you explore the Buddha image and the life of the person who inspired it, be aware of the changes in your inner life and relationships. Are you becoming more stable, more aware, gentler, and more curious about what life offers you? How are your intellectual appreciation of the Buddha and your sense of gratitude changing? Give attention to these positive changes, for they are evidence that you are moving towards realizing what the image truly represents.

6. The chapter in review

- Symbols, objects, and rituals contain significance in themselves, but that significance is augmented by what we bring to them.
- Our experience of stories changes as we change. This applies to books, films, and other pastimes, and, of course, to the spiritual life.
- Words and other symbolic representations shift in meaning on individual, linguistic, and cultural levels.
- The four levels allow us to integrate the significance of a symbol until we manifest it in our daily life. The boundary between the objective and the subjective is merged when we apply the four levels.
- An image of the Buddha, or indeed any Buddha or Bodhisattva figure, is a text. It incorporates iconography and other symbolic forms that encode meaning.

Chapter Five

Where Should Rituals Take Place?

You don't need an external temple or monastery; you've got everything within your own body.

Sangharakshita, commentary on 'The story of the yak-horn' from *The Hundred Thousand Songs of Milarepa*[33]

1. A sacred space

If you have been engaging with the 'Something to try' sections in each chapter, you will have visited a Buddhist centre or temple. There may even be a new image of the Buddha in your home, or a new way of appreciating the one you already have. By this point, you will have a sense that Buddhists don't consider statues of this nature to be just ornamentation or home decor: they are placed in special locations – on a shrine or altar, or in some other sacred place. But what makes a place sacred?

The word 'sacred' might conjure images of places such as groves and grottos, or even vast churches, synagogues, and mosques. There are places in the world that have an otherworldliness that can seem beyond time as well. I have experienced this in remote Tibetan monasteries, in deep forests, and even around megalithic cairns in Britain.

When you enter a sacred place and surrender to it, what you learn within helps you meet any mundane concerns with fresh eyes upon your return to daily life. Sacred places are found in our world, yet they are connected to something adjacent or transcendent. I vividly recall entering York Minster in a tight, miserly state of mind, and having that pettiness dissolve into the bright yet cavernous interior. My concerns were dwarfed, if not by God, then by the sublime architecture on display. To enter this sacred place was to put myself in a realm beyond myself. Are there any places you have visited that you consider sacred?

Think back to your experience of visiting a Buddhist centre or temple. Recall the artefacts and how they were displayed. By now you will be aware that the statues, shrines, flowers, and artworks, the bowls and bells and braziers of incense, do not endow a place with sacredness. In the previous chapter, I highlighted that it is how one views these objects and the practices in which they are used that provides them with power. They are ingredients in the recipe but not the dish itself, and certainly not the taste. It is the mind that makes a place sacred, the attitude that one takes towards the space that empowers both it and the objects contained within.

2. Unpacking a shrine

In Chapter 2, we established a definition of ritual by combining ideas from Erich Fromm and Dimitris Xygalatas. To reiterate, a ritual is *shared action, expressive of common strivings, rooted in shared values.*

Let's unpack a shrine room in terms of this definition:

1. What are the shared actions we engage in here, and what actions are excluded from a shrine room?
2. What might be the common strivings practised in the space?
3. What might be the shared values of those who inhabit this space?

Take some time to reflect on these questions for yourself.

Despite being ostensibly a place of stillness and silence, a shrine room is a place of activity. We remove shoes, bow, arrange our bodies in a variety of postures, and recite words in different languages all before we begin to delve inwards. By the time we have entered a shrine room, we have engaged in a plethora of actions rooted in common strivings.

I find the removal of shoes to be a ritual that is deserving of more attention. It is one of those 'that's what you do' rituals that everyone attending a Buddhist centre participates in. Like many other rituals (and it is a ritual if you consider the following elements), it has the potential to open the practitioner up.

At the most pragmatic and fundamentally mundane level, we leave shoes behind to avoid spreading dirt and keep the shrine room clean. This makes sense given how unappealing the space might be, or even how unhealthy the room could become, were we to drag in the dirt and mud from outside.

But cleanliness goes beyond the physical. In removing shoes, we are symbolically leaving behind the world where we pound the pavement looking for success, connection, and entertainment. Sneakers (or trainers) for the gym, leather brogues for work, heels for dating, boots made for walking – the kinds of shoes we wear can be determined by our occupation or financial constraints. They can also say much about the identity we seek to construct. To leave shoes aside at the entrance to a sacred space is to say, *that* identity, *that* striving, is now on hold for a time. It is a great leveller for the banker, the social media influencer, the retiree, and the lithe yogi to shuck off their shoes. Whether they are the latest Tom Ford or Jimmy Choo designs, sweat-shop-made trainers, budget Crocs knock-offs, or flip-flops, we all have the same soft and vulnerable soles once the protection of shoes has been removed. Together, unencumbered, we consciously walk on the same floor in the direction of the Buddha. Hopefully the floor is free from nails or glass or worse. Taking off our shoes is a form of renunciation of self, if only for a time.

But why do people do this? Why are they making the effort to turn up and stop doing what they normally do out there in the world? There are common themes to why people come to a Buddhist centre to meditate, but that commonality does not diminish the significance of the individual act. We may attend to begin a process of self-improvement or self-discovery. It may be that we wish to open to others more effectively or reduce our stress levels. Others come to seek profound wisdom or to belong to a welcoming community of like-minded individuals. Some make the effort to turn up to let go, to strive for something greater – the motivations for practice are as diverse as the individuals who attend and the shoes they choose to wear.

Knowing that everyone around you is striving is an important consideration when entering a shrine room. This is not a church hall or a yoga studio (though of course it might be both at different times); right now it is a place to sit and shuffle closer towards one's ideal, however one might envisage it. Through these actions of removing shoes and being quiet and still, we are setting up certain conditions not just for ourselves but for those around us. By being silent and still, we encourage others to do the same, and thus reduce the distractions that plague meditators.

Our actions have consequences that go beyond ourselves. Essentially, when we arrive in a shrine room, we are enacting the very principle of karma – actions have consequences. How we behave, how we act in that space, impacts upon ourselves and others. Our actions either support the deep aspirations and value held by others or they work against them.

What might those values be? The other practitioners might value awareness, kindness, patience, and clarity. Perhaps they value stillness and silence, or even the aesthetics of the space in which they find themselves. It could be that, like yourself, they value persistence and perseverance.

But there is something else being enacted and embodied here. Barefoot, we approach the Buddha on the shrine as kings, queens, and farmers approached the Buddha millennia ago. The Buddha image sits at the end of the room, raised up to signify his importance in the lives of practitioners. The view of the Buddha is unimpeded as we sit in orderly rows just as the first disciples did. We stand and sit so that all may see the figure of the Buddha. This is a kind of historical re-enactment of the thousands of similar meetings the Buddha had in his lifetime. To enter a shrine room is to imaginatively place oneself in the position of devotees across time who put aside worldly concerns to learn from him.

This action of reverence is happening concurrently in Tibet, New Zealand, New Hampshire, Taiwan, and London. The aesthetics may differ, but there will be a sacred space, a Buddha, faces turned towards him, and reverence. The props may be different – a wooden fish in China, an upturned skull cup in Nepal, a crystal stupa in Myanmar, a blank wall in Kyoto, a book by Jon Kabat-Zinn in Massachusetts, drooping gerberas in Sydney – but the purpose of these props is the same: each is a condition to draw one closer to the enlightened mind, whether that is seen as within, without, or transcending dualism altogether.

We've already explored the long tradition of ritual in the timeline of Buddhism, but there are rituals that date back to the Buddha himself. As the early texts indicate, when people met the Buddha, they bowed out of respect and made the anjali mudra[34] as a way of beautifying the space, purifying their intent, and practising generosity of spirit. Bowing before the Buddha in the shrine room continues that re-enactment of what has been done for thousands of years. Considering this can move one out of a personal development model into a less limited and restricted mindset. You are among billions of individuals who have done this very same practice in innumerable shrine rooms across the centuries. One is indeed part of a continuity of practice dating back to the fifth or sixth century BCE.

Lastly, when you come and sit before the Buddha and make your own efforts, based on what matters most to you, you are also bringing with you whatever concerns you deeply. Whatever trials you are facing in your life, which you might consider your own unique flavour of suffering, are present with you as you bow and as you sit. It is worth considering that the shame, guilt, anger, pride, or despair you bring is not unique, and nor are you the first to bear it in attention in a shrine room. Take confidence in the knowledge that the very concept of a shrine room, regardless of its size, design, or aesthetic, offers the potential to contain and transform whatever you have brought with you.

3. Body, speech, and mind

Let's examine the ritual of salutation to the Buddha, where people bow or make prostrations. Practitioners may stand or kneel, and quietly recite three sounds before bowing towards the shrine. These sounds may be internal rather than chanted aloud, though in some traditions they are intoned quite loudly. This is the salutation of *om*, *ah*, and *hum*.

The syllables themselves appear in many other contexts too. *Om ah hum* can be found painted on the backs of Tibetan scrolls (thangkas) to consecrate them as ritual objects as opposed to mere artworks or cultural artefacts. They are also inscribed inside statues (rupas). These objects are now said to be 'blessed', meaning that they have been set aside as devotional objects and have the potential to awaken deeper levels of practice in the owner, though only if the owner makes the effort and deeply understands the significance. An object that carries these marks is not for house decoration and design, but an object to help inspire one to make spiritual progress.

There is also a breathing technique known as vase or vajra breathing, in which one uses each of the sound syllables at different stages of breathing. This has a calming and unifying effect when practised over time. This practice is one that allows you to fully integrate body, speech, and mind around the breath. It is similar to some other breathing meditations found in different Buddhist traditions. You mentally recite *om* on breathing in, *ah* in the gap between breaths, and *hum* on the out-breath.[35]

Within some forms of Tibetan practice, *om ah hum* is inscribed by the finger on offering bowls filled with water (more on that in the next chapter) with the intention of purifying (*om*), magnifying the amount of and the meaning behind the offering (*ah*), and then reflecting on the empty nature of the offering and the one who offers (*hum*).[36]

Most commonly in a Triratna Buddhist centre, you will hear these syllables chanted before bowing to the shrine. The three syllables are repeated, and their places on the body (head, throat, and heart) are touched by joined palms. These gestures are often followed by a bow or even a full-body prostration as a sign of complete supplication to the Buddha, his teaching, and the community of practitioners. This act is one of profound humility and reverence.

When you try this for yourself, what is alive for you? What arises in the mind and heart?

Bowing before a statue might be problematic for some, particularly if the experience seems idolatrous and pagan or overly religious. Are we bowing to the actual statue, as if it contained a spirit or a god? Is this a form of animism?

Approaching Enlightenment

The statue is most definitely not a god, nor does it contain any special spirit other than what we see in it thanks to the artist's skill. It is, however, a powerful symbol with multiple layers of meaning, as we saw in the previous chapter. And it can evoke the qualities of the Buddha. This statue is a representation of the historical Buddha or another manifestation of Enlightenment. We orient ourselves towards it and put ourselves below it. But this is just one way of seeing the object.

4. More than just a bow

The salutation of *om ah hum* also has multiple levels of meaning. On a basic level, it is about being present in body (*om*), speech (*ah*), and mind (*hum*), and directing the whole of oneself towards the Buddha. This is not wrong, but there is more to it.

We return to the beginning of the journey, informed as we are by the four levels. We have removed our shoes and arrived in the shrine room, and are bowing before the image of the Buddha and reciting *om ah hum*. Let's explore this simple Buddhist ritual through the four levels of experiencing, understanding, applying, and realizing.

Experiencing *om*

This Sanskrit syllable is usually depicted as white – the colour is sometimes described as the white of sunlight on snow, suggesting that it is reflective of Enlightenment, not synonymous with it. *Om* evokes purity, calm, and peace. The sound of *om* can be delivered in a slow, sonorous way, or it can be abrupt and punchy. Hearing it has an impact, a vibration that can be pleasant and evoke the qualities of spaciousness or energy.

Understanding *om*

When we chant *om* before a shrine in salutation, we align our body in the direction of Enlightenment – we face the Buddha image as we chant this. We are acknowledging the universal truth he rediscovered – the truth of conditioned co-production. In simple terms, this is stating that all phenomena come into being in dependence on conditions.

This syllable is often found at the beginning of mantras to indicate that what follows arises from that pure, unsullied state of *om*. Before all things, *om* suggests, is a primordial purity out of which the body of the universe arises. *Om* also refers to our own body, a physical body that arises in dependence upon certain conditions. Like the sound, our bodies arise and pass away.

Lama Govinda, Sangharakshita's contemporary and friend, wrote that *om* is far more than an acknowledgement of the body: *om* is 'the seed-syllable of the universe',[37] which points to the continuous spontaneous arising of matter and of consciousness. The universe, from a Buddhist perspective, is seen as one of physical matter, but matter permeated with consciousness. Consciousness and matter intertwined! Consciousness or mind is not seen as a by-product of the brain.

Om is an acknowledgement of the universe of matter and consciousness of which we are a part. In reciting *om*, one is opening one's arms and embracing all that exists.[38]

Applying *om*

To recite and repeat *om* is to be open to the totality of existence with full knowledge that phenomena arise and pass in dependence upon conditions. Reciting the syllable is an opportunity to apply conditionality in one's favour, to shape a new existence from this sound syllable onwards, from this action onwards, from this moment onwards. Here we can see how the consequences of skilful actions purify and refine consciousness.

To recite *om* is to purify the actions of the body, and to dedicate the actions of the body to the welfare of all beings. Chanting *om* with awareness can bring an ethical sensitivity to what our body does and can do. This is then refined with the subsequent syllable *ah*.

The syllable itself does not purify us – that would be to wrongly consider *om* as a magic spell. It is the intention we bring to act with greater purity of heart and to be more ethical that we are affirming when we chant this sound with full awareness. We begin to see the interplay between our own actions, those of others, and the world.

Realizing *om*

To realize *om* is to live with the perception that phenomena are inherently pure and undefiled because no phenomenon has a fixed, unchanging form. Nothing is solid or permanent, though it appears as such. The apparent form of things is by its very nature changing. The body we exhibit is in flux. Our experiences and the experiences of others are also in a state of constant change or becoming. To unify with *om* is to be totally at peace with the ever-changing nature of life. *Om* is an open, accepting receptivity to all that is. This is a state synonymous with deep and profound equanimity.

Would you like to experience life in this way?

Experiencing *ah*

This syllable is red. In the Tibetan script, it includes two small circles on the side, which indicate it is a long, extended sound, like *aaaahhhh*. Its redness is redolent with energy, emotion, passion even. This connects to the way in which the sound is made. It is sometimes similar to the 'Ah!' that one makes when realizing something in a eureka moment – 'Ah hah! That's the answer!' Sometimes *ah* is more breathy, soft, and mysterious. When chanted in this manner, it is much more a sound of release.

Understanding *ah*

Ah represents our speech and thought at their best. In fact, *ah* is the sound of our very first utterance – our first cry as a newborn baby. Thus, by association, *ah* is an opportunity to begin again, to start communicating to ourselves and others in a more pure and wholesome manner. (Coming as this does directly after *om*, it is flavoured by the same purity.)

Communication arises in dependence on both the physical body and the mind. Intention, lungs, tongue, mouth, and breath come together to form sound. Again, *ah* is a reminder that all we think and say arises from factors that are themselves conditioned. Nothing exists in isolation.

We can choose to attune our speech to be in line with our ideals and ethics. What are the words we put out into the world? Is our speech in alignment with what we hold dear? There are a number of Buddhist precepts and practices associated with speech. Speech is pure and wholesome if it is true, kindly, encouraging, harmonious, and relevant. (See Chapter 8 for more on this.)

This syllable is associated with certain Buddhist figures of devotion like the Buddha of unobstructed activity or success, Amoghasiddhi. Just like the actions of Buddha Amoghasiddhi, our words have the capacity to create new realities. Our words can forge long-lasting bonds, elucidate the great mysteries of science, and weave new cultural artefacts. Conversely, they can tear others down, design weapons of mass destruction, and incite bigotry. Words, and the thoughts that precede them, create worlds when they are released from our mouths.

In some Tibetan traditions, *ah* is used to magnify the amount of offerings. For example, if one is motivated by faith and confidence to make an offering but one doesn't have the means to make an elaborate gift, the syllable *ah* might be transcribed on the object or recited over it to honour the intensity of feeling. *Ah* is seen to transform the simple offering into a treasure.

Applying *ah*

Consider the power of speech to spread beyond the utterance of the original speaker. One sentence spoken by an individual is heard by multiple ears and reproduced in the mind, and then may be passed on to others. For example, in the presence of others a person might say, 'We must stand up for those who cannot do so for themselves.' Even as the words are said, they are received and interpreted in the minds of those present. The words spoken by one person are suddenly multiplied by the number of listeners. The words are passed on. Just as sound begins in one mind and is released through utterance, thus entering the minds of many, we can magnify and multiply our spoken actions for the benefit of all beings. As an offering, we can lend our voice to be of service to others.

It is therefore important that we offer words that align with the best in us. Words have impact. What impact does your speech have on yourself, others, and the world? Inner communication is relevant here – self-talk, as the world of psychology puts it. How do you speak to yourself about yourself? Are you hypercritical or overly praising? And how do you speak of others? Is there a disparity between what you think of others and what you actually say to them?

The syllable *ah* stands for what magnifies and intensifies. Moreover, it represents a movement from pure existence into the realm of ethical action, particularly as it pertains to speech. Do you speak truthfully and in a helpful manner? Do your words inspire others to be their best? Does what you are saying absolutely need to be said now, or at all? Above all, do you speak with kindness at the fore? Applying speech precepts (see Chapter 8 for more on this topic) can help you realize the power of *ah*.

Realizing *ah*

To contemplate *ah* is to know deeply the magic of reality. The evolution of words over time facilitates communication, yet a word is not the thing it describes. Neither is the sound of that word; yet both conjure the meaning to the mind as we saw in the previous chapter. Sounds and words point to reality in a way similar to the Zen master pointing at the moon, where the finger is the teaching, and the moon is Enlightenment itself.

To fully penetrate *ah*, one realizes that a simple utterance can raise someone up or send them to the depths of depression. Words clearly have power despite their ephemeral, ambiguous, and illusory nature.

Ah encompasses the apparently real and simultaneously phantom-like nature of phenomena. Object described, senses contacting, memory accessed, mouth and tongue forming, breath used, person to whom one directs the sound – these are but some of the conditions that need to come into play when any word is said. It is an astonishing phantom, a complex illusion that we conjure each time we speak.

Can you see the world in this way? Do you speak and think with this degree of discernment regarding the miracle of speech?

Experiencing *hum*

Hum is a complex symbol that is actually an aggregate of several parts. Some traditions see three, others discern five discrete segments to the symbol in the Tibetan script. *Hum* is not pronounced *hum* as in the word 'humming' – it is more of a *hoong*, with an elongated *m* that sounds like a nasal *ng*, as in *sing* or *ring*. The sound is deep, resonant, and extended.

The syllable is blue, which suggests the openness of the sky or the shifting, shimmering beauty of the ocean, though, as you will see below, within the Indo-Tibetan system of colour associations, there are some surprising connections.

This sound syllable can often be found at the end of mantras to indicate a conclusion, an ending, or even a lesson learned.

Understanding *hum*

The colour blue has contradictory associations within Buddhism. On the one hand, it is the blue of the sky: open and unobstructed, and unaffected by the clouds that at times obscure it. Sky blue is suggestive of possibilities and freedom. It is also connected to the soothing quality of water, which can extinguish the fires of hatred. On the other hand, if the blue is a darker shade (as *hum* often is), the connotation is more forceful, almost wrathful. This is the blue of strong, decisive, and even potentially aggressive figures like Vajrapani or Mahakala (whom we will meet later in the book). This particular blue communicates the power of dedication and determination to overcome obstacles.

Lama Govinda links *hum* to the image of the Buddha touching the earth at the moment before Enlightenment as a sign of his aeons of practice. At this moment, the Buddha calls on the earth itself to give testimony of the Buddha's tenacity and fortitude. So, in reciting this, we are called to commit ourselves and to acknowledge the efforts we have made again and again to come to this very moment of devotion.

This sparks another fascinating association. Just as the historical Buddha touches the earth, he recollects the millennia of practice that went before – he unites past and present. Moreover, the past is endless and the moment of touching is a fixed point: *hum* is a unification of polar opposites. Lama Govinda says it best and in a more poetic manner:

> *Hum* is the infinite in the finite, the eternal in the temporal, the timeless in the moment, the unconditioned in the conditioned, the formless as basis of all form.[39]

Hum is frequently equated with the mind, with our volitions, thoughts, cognitions, emotions, knowledge, and intentions. Compared to the syllables *om* and *ah*, *hum* is the most personal of the syllables because it points to our very sense of identity, particularly the aspect of ourselves that strives for freedom. At the same time, as Lama Govinda remarks, we note that there is a higher, transpersonal self that exists beyond the confines of the physical. This is a mystery that can only be penetrated through direct experience.

At its simplest, *hum* directs all that remains of our sense of being towards the goal of freedom. In reciting it here, we are laying this striving bare.

Applying *hum*

Hum is a reminder to be fully committed and authentic. It's not enough to go though the motions – to use the body and speech to practise; our mind or will must be in alignment with every other part of ourselves. *Hum* is the aspiration to grow amidst the mess of a disorganized mind. *Hum* is the entirety of our inner experience turning to the ideal of Enlightenment.

Our mind is a potent manifestation of conditioned co-production. Things arise within the mind in dependence upon conditions and, in turn, dissolve back into the mind. Just like external phenomena that appear to come together and fall apart. The mind is constant but ever-changing. There is nothing solid on which to hold when you look to the mind. Watch for yourself. Is there any internal phenomenon, any thought or emotion, that remains static and unchanging?

Everything you experience, from the pain of a splinter to the latest cinematic spectacle, arises in the mind. Without the mind to weave together the pieces (and the senses that take in the pieces in the first place), there is no picture of the world or of yourself. Is that true? Can you have an experience that is separated from or distinct from your own perception mitigated by your mind? Mind is the fundamental building block of your experience. How do you treat your mind? How do you feed your mind?

Chanting *hum* in this context is to draw a line in the sand, to place your flag or standard in the ground and say, 'I turn my mind towards Enlightenment and liberation.' It is a statement of purpose, of intent.

Realizing *hum*

To fully manifest *hum* is to fully commit oneself to the path, or go for refuge to the Buddha, the Dharma, and the Sangha. (For more on this, see Chapter 8.) To realize *hum*, one must live with the experience of the entire world, both outer and inner, as a product of the mind. All phenomena are empty of inherent existence, and are in a flow of constant change. This includes our own sense of identity, the habit we have of being a certain person who behaves in a certain way. (The fetter of habit is fastening tighter again.) To live in the realm of *hum* is to know deeply from experience that suffering arises when we cling to the shifting sands and expect them to be solid, real, and permanent. We choose to not be guided by this clinging. This is the luminous and unsullied mind of a Buddha.

5. Something to try

Within the material above, there may be elements that ring true, and others that arise as a challenge. Take these on for contemplation, and leave the rest for another time. There is no expectation that you need to bring every level of association to your mind each time you bow to a shrine – such mental activity would be an impediment to the purpose. Instead, be selective and curious. Be receptive, not analytical. Informed with the knowledge, see what transpires as you recite *om ah hum* and bow.

If you have a space in which you meditate and have a home shrine, take time to recite the following salutation to the Buddha, and perhaps even bow:

namo Buddhaya	Homage to the Buddha – enlightened one
namo Dharmaya	Homage to the Dharma – teachings
namo Sanghaya	Homage to the Sangha – community of enlightened disciples
namo nama	Emphatically so
om ah hum	With body With speech With heart / mind

If you don't have a designated shrine space in which to chant, consider setting one up. It need not be elaborate or expensive, but it needs to have a clear purpose, even if it must be collapsed at the end of each session. The basic items you need are an image of the Buddha (which you will now have, after our earlier exploration) and a place to sit either facing it or to one side. How you ornament the space is up to you at this stage. As this book proceeds, there will be some suggestions of what might be suitable to include as you build up your ritual practice.

When you bow to the shrine you have set up, reflect on the significance of the Buddha in your own life. Consider what arises within as you perform such a practice – is it embarrassing, is it an intellectual response, a growing stillness, something emotional in nature, or none of the above? Witness your honest response without judgement. The attentiveness is all.

That said, reach within for what you are thankful for or curious about in this new world of Buddhism you have ventured into. Foster that response. To connect more deeply

to the seed syllables of *om ah hum,* you could engage with
the practice of vajra breathing outlined above, as a variation
on the mindfulness of breathing practice.

Here the practice is described in more detail:

1. Settle into your posture, the intention for the practice,
   and the breath.
2. Let go of effort and rest in your posture. Do not try to
   grasp at any experience or result.
3. On the natural in-breath, recite *om* internally. It could be
   the sound alone or even a visual of the syllable. As you
   breathe in, the *om* rides the entirety of the breath.
4. In the gap between the in- and out-breath, allow the
   ah to rest, even if it is only for a brief moment. You do
   not need to elongate the gap. Again, you can rest in the
   sound and/or the image of the syllable. Be careful not to
   control the experience, creating a certain identity, a self.
5. *Hum* rides the natural, uncontrived out-breath into the
   silence before the next *om.* Again, the *hum* (pronounced
   hoong) lasts the entirety of the out-breath.
6. Repeat this for a few cycles as you begin to settle into
   a gentle uncontrived rhythm. Should the experience
   become tight or mechanical, just stop and rest in the
   natural flow of the breath without the syllables.

6. The chapter in review

Perhaps now you have a clearer sense of what forms the sanctity of
place and where rituals can happen. Take time to reflect on your own
answer, maybe even recording those thoughts in a journal. These are
some of the elements that create a sacred space:

- an acknowledgement that sacredness is evoked in the
  interaction between intention, object, and space;
- a positive intention to be open, receptive, and curious;

- the inclusion of symbolic objects that evoke connection to one's highest ideals;
- expressing gratitude for a path of practice and the Buddha;
- repeatedly applying oneself to the practices one has been taught;
- some knowledge of the significance of these items and practices;
- an awareness of how conditioned co-production is at play at all times.

Chapter Six

Worship: How Much Am I Prepared to Give?

The seven offerings of the Mahayana represent our response. When the transcendental appears and takes us by surprise, we drop everything and attend only to the transcendental, to the Buddha. That undivided attention is expressed by giving the best we have, not holding back but giving everything we have, giving out of unbounded gratitude, unbounded love, and joy.

Sangharakshita, *Creative Symbols of Tantric Buddhism*[40]

1. Ten thousand Buddhas are not enough

In the early phases of Buddhist practice, you might not be prepared to make offerings, except perhaps of money for books or courses on meditation. But there is something you might be prepared to do other than offering cash. I'd like to illustrate this with a personal story.

In the year 2000, I was hit with a stick by a Buddhist nun. This was in the middle of a silent meditation retreat; in fact, it was during an actual meditation session! To be fair, I deserved it, as I was a poor student and rubbish at staying awake in meditation. She wielded the wooden sword (the wake-up stick) with pinpoint accuracy as she whacked my back. I was immediately thrust into a heightened sense of awareness with only the faintest of shoulder pain where she hit her mark.

This was an auspicious day. This retreat culminated in a lay ordination! I was resplendent in black robes and a brown 'cassock', along with 300 Taiwanese devotees. Mine was one of very few Caucasian faces. I was becoming a Buddhist, and had no idea what that meant.

As we processed into a shine room that was so large you could almost use it as an aircraft hangar, I was in awe of the five enormous Buddhas that dwarfed us. They wore different coloured robes, but had uniform expressions of curiosity. Every remaining centimetre of the walls was filled with miniature Buddhas, all with little LED lights pulsing.

The shrine laid out before us was stacked high with objects and elaborate offerings presented by devotees. Stacks of fruit were piled like champagne flutes on display at a celebrity wedding. Gongs, wooden instruments, bamboo in ceramic pots, and elaborate lanterns shaped like lotus flowers were positioned carefully, each attended by a nun in red and gold brocade robes. I was in awe of the exotic treasures before me.

But then the translator's voice in my earpiece informed me I should bow. And so I did, tripping on the hem of my robes. I careened into an older woman, whose look of disdain I can still recall vividly. I was never quite in sync with my bows. Around me, hundreds were apparently 'going for refuge', whatever that was. We bowed a lot, I remember. In between bows, I caught glimpses of gongs being hit and objects being waved about. I so wanted to wave them about too! I had no idea what was happening or what the objects were, but my oh my, did I feel special! It was a magical day.

My partner, who was without an earpiece or a translator, was less than impressed, because the ceremony continued for three hours! He had not consented to becoming a Buddhist, but that is what had inadvertently happened to him, along with the rest of the people in the shrine room. As the crowds surged forward to be splashed with water by the grand master, my partner was swept up into the congregation and ritually anointed! We had both committed to becoming Buddhas one day. No pressure! Now there was potential for two more Buddhas in the world. He was very silent on the long drive home in the car.

Looking back at that time, I am filled with embarrassment that I was prepared to go through something so significant and elaborate without any real awareness of the meaning or the consequences. I was a tourist having an exotic foreign experience. But mostly what concerned me at the time was that I wanted to get one of the large wooden fish instruments that make a *tok tok* sound when you hit them. I had to get that on my shrine at home. Once I had a shrine, of course. Had to buy one of those first.

Becoming a Buddhist (if this is indeed what had happened that long day) had not reduced my greed for acquisition. I might not have been prepared to give, but I certainly was prepared to buy!

Some years later, in 2003 to be precise, I understood the potential of true going for refuge at a simple ceremony in a room with one rather unimpressive brass Buddha and no wooden fish. That day I brought with me three offerings purchased locally – an orange dahlia, a citrus-scented candle, and some noxious cheap sandalwood incense. I knew the meaning of these offerings, both from the tradition and from my own heart. I offered them to a simple shrine, and the direction of my life changed completely. This shrine was worth more to me than 10,000 Buddhas and strobing LED lights. I had gone for refuge, and continue to do so to this day.

2. Three offerings

Let's have a fresh look at a more modest Buddhist shrine and its many symbolic items. They may be less exotic than those I experienced in the year 2000, but, in knowing their meaning, I am better equipped to become what they represent.

Rather than launch into an analysis of the components one finds on a shrine, we can engage in a ritual that addresses some of the items directly. The Threefold Puja is a ritual that was composed by Urgyen Sangharakshita for the Triratna Buddhist Community in Finland.

At present this puja is in the process of being translated into other languages. It now exists in Hebrew, Chinese, Portuguese, Esperanto, Afrikaans, Japanese, Albanian, Thai, and many other languages.[41]

'Puja' means 'act of worship'; a puja can be simple or elaborate, depending on the form, time constraints, and inclination of those involved. 'Threefold', in this instance, refers to the fact that the liturgy or verses are arranged in three parts, three distinct phases. The puja begins with reverence, an attitude of respect and admiration. This reverence is then directed more precisely towards the Three Jewels, the three highest qualities or strands of the Buddhist path. Lastly, offerings are made to the Three Jewels, providing an opportunity to reflect and gain insight.

Let's be clear: when we worship the Buddha, we are not praising him in order to avoid his displeasure or judgement. Also, we are not praying to him for forgiveness. We are not bowing to seek his intervention in our lives. It is not a transactional relationship in that sense. To worship in a Buddhist sense is not to gain but to give, to release one's grasping to anything whatsoever, even receiving dividends or results. Sangharakshita makes this point unequivocally when he asserts that puja is essentially 'an act of giving, not of receiving'.[42]

Yet it is ironic how much one gains by giving. To discover that, you need to practise puja rather than have it explained to you. To that end, I suggest that you take on a regular practice of the Threefold Puja for a time. Commit to practising it a certain number of times a week for a few weeks. Daily would be best, but whatever you decide – be realistic given the details of your life.

Before taking it on as a practice, read the text of the puja to experience it and then to contemplate the meaning. This is an opportunity to engage the more rational aspect of yourself with the text. Consider it carefully, and note any questions or objections you might have. If you can, think about addressing these with an Order member or fellow Buddhist you trust and respect. Then, once you are prepared, take this on for a period.

Begin by setting up a shrine and a space in which to direct your energies/aspiration. Salute the shrine as described in the last chapter, and then sit in silence to gather yourself and your intentions. It may prove beneficial to meditate before and after the ritual for as long as you have time.

When an Order member is present, it is customary to have them lead the verses in call and response. Recite the words after the speaker, and reflect on the meaning of those words and of that action for you. If you are alone, it is perfectly acceptable to read the verses yourself.

The Threefold Puja

1. Opening reverence

We reverence the Buddha, the Perfectly Enlightened One,
the Shower of the Way.

We reverence the Dharma, the Teaching of the Buddha,
which leads from darkness to Light.

We reverence the Sangha, the fellowship of the Buddha's
disciples, that inspires and guides.

2. Reverence to the Three Jewels

We reverence the Buddha, and aspire to follow Him.
The Buddha was born as we are born.
What the Buddha overcame, we too can overcome;
What the Buddha attained, we too can attain.

We reverence the Dharma, and aspire to follow it
With body, speech, and mind until the end.
The Truth in all its aspects, the Path in all its stages,
We aspire to study, practise, realize.

We reverence the Sangha, and aspire to follow it:
The fellowship of those who tread the Way.
As, one by one, we make our own commitment,
An ever-widening circle, the Sangha grows.

3. Offerings to the Buddha

Reverencing the Buddha, we offer flowers:
Flowers that today are fresh and sweetly blooming,
Flowers that tomorrow are faded and fallen.
Our bodies too, like flowers, will pass away.

Reverencing the Buddha, we offer candles:
To Him, who is the Light, we offer light.
From His greater lamp a lesser lamp we light within us:
The lamp of Bodhi shining within our hearts.
Reverencing the Buddha, we offer incense:

Incense whose fragrance pervades the air.
The fragrance of the perfect life, sweeter than incense,
Spreads in all directions throughout the world.

There may be some terms in the puja that are unfamiliar. What follows is a brief glossary to assist.

> *Reverence*: respect, admiration, and even awe that one directs actively towards that which one holds in high esteem. It begins with gratitude and moves from there, into faith or confidence in the teaching.
>
> *Truth*: this is not conventional truth as in right or wrong, true or false – it refers to the understanding of the Buddha, his insight or wisdom. At its simplest and most principial, the truth the Buddha realized was that phenomena arise in dependence upon conditions, and, in the absence of those conditions, phenomena do not arise. This applies across all aspects of reality as we know it, both externally and internally.
>
> *Path*: this refers to the noble eightfold path, which lays out the blueprint for a Buddhist life, though it also refers to the many other formulations that guide individuals towards Enlightenment.[43]
>
> *Bodhi*: this translates as 'Enlightenment' or 'Awakening'.
> A 'lamp of Bodhi' refers to the potential we all have to kindle the flame of Enlightenment. One way of describing Enlightenment is as freedom from the fetters.

3. Reflections on the Threefold Puja

After conducting the puja a few times, ask yourself the following questions:

1. What are your thoughts having completed the ritual?
2. Did this response develop or change as you repeated the practice?
3. To what extent were you engaged emotionally, imaginatively, and intellectually?

4. What have you actually given?
5. Has anything been gained?

Here are some thoughts on the questions and on the Threefold Puja to add to your own:

- There are several elements of this modern text that are striking. Firstly, there is a dynamism in it, an inherent sense of movement. The Buddha shows the way. He guides and leads us. We are cast in the role of seekers, of travellers who are leaving behind what holds us back and moving into his sphere of influence. Puja is thus active, not passive. This harks back to the image of the Buddha and us as the magician, actively exploring reality.

- Secondly, the puja dispenses with the individual 'I' in favour of the collective 'we'. We practise puja as individuals, making our own personal commitment, but alongside a community of others. This is an illustration of Fromm's 'common striving': we are *applying* ourselves alongside others, beside others, for others. The spiritual life is thus a collegial and collective one, despite the individual efforts that are made. This collective aspiration becomes a source of confidence and support – we are not alone.

- Thirdly, the puja affirms our potential. We can become enlightened. This is not questioned. Regardless of what you bring with you to the shrine room, if you practise wholeheartedly to break the chains that restrain you, Enlightenment is your inheritance.

The offerings serve more than a decorative function – they have the potential to bring us to insight. By offering flowers to the Buddha, we acknowledge the transitory nature of beauty and the impermanence of all things. By offering candles, we can see that our actions can illuminate faults and virtues alike. Not just our minds but our hearts are illuminated. That is significant. Lastly, incense is offered. Our actions impact and condition the lives of those around us. One incense stick can enliven an entire room with its scent. We can all be united in the fragrance of compassionate action.

The Dharma verse in the second section also echoes the four levels we explored previously. We reverence the Dharma by outwardly bowing towards the shrine (outer level – experiencing). We study it by learning and remembering (inner level – understanding). We practise it (secret/hidden level – applying) and we realize its meaning (ultimate level – realizing).

4. The nature of offerings

The Buddha does not need your offerings. Again, the statue is not a god or a deity that needs to be appeased with offerings. These offerings are not given to curry favour with the Buddha, but to bring oneself imaginatively into the presence of the Buddha – to re-enact what was done over 2,000 years ago.

Consider the offerings as preparation for an honoured guest or friend you are welcoming into your home. It is still customary to clean one's living quarters for a guest and provide nourishment, comfort, and entertainment for them. This, on one level, is what we are doing when making offerings to a shrine.

What do you offer an honoured guest when they come to visit? Do you provide drinks and snacks? Maybe you freshen up the decor with flowers and something scented, like a candle or incense? To receive a guest takes care and preparation.

On the outer level (as we saw in Chapter 4 on the four levels), when we make offerings, we are preparing the space for the Buddha with a series of special gifts. These in turn have more universal meanings, as we shall see.

The traditional offerings in the Indo-Tibetan tradition[44] are:

1. water for drinking to quench the thirst;
2. water for washing the face, feet, and hands;
3. flowers to beautify the space and the mind;
4. incense to purify the air (and also remove distracting insects);
5. lights to dispel the dark, and so guests can see each other and talk long into the night;

6. scented water to make guests smell pleasant and feel refreshed;
7. food to eat to nourish and sustain;
8. music to entertain and engage the heart.

These would be offered to the Buddha in his time, and are still offered to shrines all over the Buddhist world. There are practices ranging from the simple to the highly elaborate involving these offerings. Tibetan traditions say one can simply fill the bowls with water in the morning and empty them at night (though not a drop of water is allowed to remain in the emptied bowls). This symbolic offering can also be taken to extremes, with the creation of highly realistic representations of offerings made from dough or even butter.

Many Buddhist centres within the Triratna tradition will have seven or eight bowls on a shrine. Sometimes they might contain candles or tea lights. At other times they might simply contain water or rice. Of course, these offerings have greater significance, but first we need to consider just what exactly is being given when one prepares these offerings to the shrine.

Firstly, the offerings serve no functional purpose: the statue or the people present in the room do not need or use them in any way, yet care is given in the presentation and execution of the offerings. Time is dedicated to giving for the sake of giving. Giving without expectation of return is the key here. Offerings are given purely to practise giving. This is an act of selflessness, of generosity at its purest.

Secondly, there is an aesthetic quality to the care with which one prepares the offerings. They do create a certain ambience. The precision with which you present the bowls says as much about your practice of mindfulness as it does about your artistic sense. That said, there is much to appreciate in an aesthetically pleasing shrine layout. Such devotion can enable others to become more present, and more dedicated to practice.

Below is a table that lays out the traditional offerings and how you might think of them in terms of the four levels.

Word/outer meaning	General/inner meaning
Experiencing	*Understanding*
	Water for drinking To quench the guest's thirst after the journey
	Water for washing To soothe the tired feet and wash away the dirt/dust
Seven (or, more rarely, eight) offering bowls laid out before the Buddha or Bodhisattva image on the shrine.	Flowers To beautify the space and the mind – a sign of respect and admiration in Indian culture
The bowls, whether full or empty, represent the offerings one gives to an honoured guest according to ancient Indian custom.	Incense To cleanse the air and ward off insects
The guest may arrive unannounced, requiring you to drop everything and attend to their needs.	Lights To brighten the room so one may see others clearly and talk into the night
	Scented water To freshen the face, hands, and body
	Food To sustain the guest and give them strength
	Music To entertain and gladden the mind/heart

Hidden/secret meaning	Ultimate meaning
Applying	*Realizing*
To what extent do I reduce thirst/craving and grasping in my life? Do I exemplify such renunciation to others?	All beings experience the suffering brought on by thirsting for experience and existence. What truly alleviates that craving?
To what extent do I engage in meritorious, other-oriented actions that reduce suffering?	All beings are caked in the consequences of their actions throughout time, throughout a multitude of lives. Skilful action removes this 'dirt'.
Do I see the delicate, transcendent beauty in life, and offer that perspective to others?	All things arise and pass away – impermanence is the only constant. Beauty is in the fragility and transience.
Am I working on living a more ethical life to reduce greed, hatred, and delusion in the world?	Ethical actions purify and remove the hindrances to gaining Enlightenment.
Am I a light for others? Do I work to be an exemplar?	The Dharma itself is a light in the darkness of samsara for us and for others.
Is my practice alive, fresh, and inspiring to others?	Meditation and meritorious actions can soothe discomfort.
Do I offer to others what they need? Do I receive what I need to sustain practice?	A middle way between indulgence and abstinence can sustain us.
Am I able to dwell in positive, uplifting mental states and encourage others to dwell in them too?	There is an intangible beauty to a life of Dharma practice if one gives it attention.

These offerings are sometimes made purely in words or even in hand gestures called mudras, though having physical offerings can help keep the practice of generosity alive. By making a variety of gestures to emulate the offering, you can enact how things arise and pass away. For example, you might make a cup-like shape by joining two hands, as if to offer a container of water to the guest. This is offered and then, when you turn your hands, the cup and the imagined water are gone. They existed, then they didn't. Then the hands make the next offering. The mudras are a physical manifestation of conditioned co-production. Each shape formed by the hands transforms into something else.

Much is made of these mudras in the Tibetan tradition. I have seen Tibetan and Bhutanese monks construct and dissolve these complex gestures – they are as beautiful as they are hypnotic. It takes hours of training just to learn the sequence, just like a dancer might learn a complex choreography. Through these ritualized movements, the practitioner can create shapes that encapsulate the entire world, which are in turn offered as a sign of devotion. The ultimate generosity is of giving one's every experience up to the Buddha, for the benefit of all living beings.

Besides the making of ritualized movements, Buddhist devotional texts lay out the requirements of a ritual offering. The opening of the Sevenfold Puja (which we will examine in detail later) evokes the seven traditional offerings. Drawing on ancient Indian customs as laid out in Shantideva's *Bodhicaryavatara*, the Sevenfold Puja (or seven-limbed prayer) makes it clear that devotion begins with ardent and selfless acts of giving:

> With mandarava, blue lotus, and jasmine,
> With all flowers pleasing and fragrant,
> And with garlands skilfully woven,
> I pay honour to the princes of the Sages,
> So worthy of veneration.
>
> I envelop them in clouds of incense,
> Sweet and penetrating;
> I make them offerings of food, hard and soft,
> And pleasing kinds of liquids to drink.

I offer them lamps, encrusted with jewels,
Festooned with golden lotus.
On the paving, sprinkled with perfume,
I scatter handfuls of beautiful flowers.[45]

5. Something to try

With a sacred space set up at home, no matter how simple
or elaborate, and with a developing sense of reverence, it is
time to begin a regular practice of puja. Any time of the day
is fine, though some prefer to begin or end the day with this
practice.

You might like to take this opportunity to add flowers,
incense, and candles to the shrine, now that you are aware
of their meaning and purpose. Then, when you have
arranged them in a pleasing manner, you can use the
questions in the 'Applying' column of the table above to
start reflecting on their significance.

Begin by saluting the shrine, as described in Chapter 5.
Then, establish yourself in a meditative and appreciatively
open state. The vajra breathing and mindfulness of
breathing practices are useful in this regard. They can assist
you in becoming more fully present. Then read the verses of
the Threefold Puja aloud. You can reflect between the verses
on what they really mean to you, and even make offerings
should you feel so moved.

Establish a plan for how and when you might practise
the Threefold Puja regularly over the coming week, and
note how you are affected each time you practise.

After each practice of the puja, take time to rest in your
response. Remember to bring patience, kindness, and
the curiosity of the magician's gaze to your experience,
whatever it is.

And a word of warning for those who, like me, are prone
to building up expectations about what should happen

during and after a puja. You might expect a calm open state, or even some grand spiritual epiphany. Positive experiences can give rise to expectations, as we grasp to have the same experiences again. We may want a certain outcome, and then feel disappointed when it does not arise. Doubt can quickly set in if we have expectations. Better to release any expectations, and instead be open to whatever arises.

6. The chapter in review

Offering is as much a state of mind as it is about giving material goods. Here is a summary of the ways to approach offerings as laid out in this chapter.

- The intent to give is foremost, particularly if it is motivated by faith or gratitude.
- The truest offerings are not transactional in nature – one offers just to give, not with the hope of receiving a blessing or boon.
- By making offerings to a shrine, you invite the Buddha and what he represents into your home and, by association, into your life.
- Making offerings can be a practice of mindfulness in and of itself.
- Offerings need not be literal representations; hand gestures and bowls can be substituted, but what cannot be replaced is the intent to give unreservedly.
- The offerings present you with reflections that may impact on how you choose to act in the world.

Chapter Seven

Salutation: What Do I Bow To?

If you leave out devotion you are closing the door on any emotional engagement with your spiritual ideal. A healthy spiritual life, just as much as a healthy psychological life, must include the expression of emotion. At the same time, there is a balance to be maintained. Faith and devotion can go to extremes, and when they do so they become superstition, fanaticism, or intolerance.

Sangharakshita, *What Is the Dharma?*[46]

1. What we all share

With a shrine set up, and a stronger appreciation of the Buddha and offerings established, you may experience feelings of calm or even gratitude. In many Asian cultures, the natural expression of gratitude and respect is to bow. In this chapter, we will go more deeply into the 'shared values' of ritual and how Buddhists seek to enact these values.

Let's return to something more direct and personal: what do you value? Health? Wellbeing? Perhaps you value freedom, parity, and fairness above all. Or are you someone who places love at the heart of all you do? Whatever your predisposition, there is something primal that unites us all, something that we all experience in a variety of forms. This isn't something we value – we do all we can to avoid it. This unifying experience we might call discomfort, or irritation, disappointment, frustration, stress, and even pain. The Buddha called this dukkha, which we often translate as 'suffering'. We all know this experience.

When we experience pain, we yearn for its passing. As children, we may be cared for by a loving parent when we are unwell. Momentary relief can be provided by a loving smile and a gentle embrace. These are acts of compassion, a love that works tirelessly and selflessly to alleviate the suffering of others. We have all benefited from acts of compassion, and all have offered compassion to another, often in unseen ways.

The word 'compassion' is derived from a fourteenth-century Latin term, *compassio*, which translates as 'suffering with another' or 'feeling together'. Middle English takes this even further by saying compassion is a 'literal sharing of affliction or suffering with another'.[47] Compassion is not a personal 'feeling' that you have in response to another's pain and discomfort: it is an empathetic sharing of the experience coupled with an urgency to alleviate it.

Within the Buddhist tradition, there are many embodiments of compassion that can appear as male, female, neither, or both. These are known as Bodhisattvas – 'Awakening beings'. These appear in human or roughly human form to suggest that deep within humanity is an essentially compassionate nature. Because of their human form, we can also identify and connect more intimately with the concepts and practices these Bodhisattvas represent. We can look into their eyes, observe the gentle smiles.

In the Sevenfold Puja, after preparing the shrine and welcoming the honoured guest, we move into cultivating a state of compassionate awareness. This is achieved through dedicating our body, speech, and mind during what is called a mantra. Frequently the mantra recited during the offerings in a Triratna Buddhist puja is the mantra of Avalokitesvara, who is called Chenrezig in Tibetan. This is not a historical figure in the way the Buddha is. Avalokitesvara is more in the realm of legend, myth, and story, which communicates a whole other degree of truth.

2. Verses that protect

But first, what is a mantra, specifically in the sphere of Buddhist practice? The word 'mantra' has entered our vernacular mostly due to the counterculture of the 1960s and, more recently, the

Approaching Enlightenment

wellness movement incorporating yoga and secular mindfulness. Transcendental Meditation (or TM, as it is often known) provides practitioners with a mantra tailored to their needs. Outside of these contexts, one might also encounter 'mantra' to mean a phrase that one says repeatedly to reflect and empower a core belief. Examples might be statements like, 'My body is a temple', 'I create my own path', 'May I love and be loved.' This everyday use of the word 'mantra' is synonymous with a personal motto or self-affirmation. Mantras in this way are akin to slogans in that they are catchy and easily remembered, and have a clear message.

It could be argued that an affirmation such as 'I create my own path' meets this definition of mantra, as it is a salient reminder that we are the active agent in our lives and, rather than succumb to peer pressure, we can take a proactive stance. Reciting this phrase, having it at the forefront of your mind, could be seen to 'work with and protect the mind'. It will most definitely have an effect. But the purpose and practice of mantra in Buddhist ritual practice are different.

The word 'mantra' is constructed of two Sanskrit syllables – *man* from *manas*, meaning 'mind', and *tra* meaning either 'protects' or 'instrumentality' (as in 'a capacity to work with', such as one might with tools). Thus, at least from a definitional perspective, a mantra refers to 'a means to work with and protect the mind'. But, given that all spiritual practices provide an opportunity to work with and, to some extent, protect the mind, this definition does not provide much focus on what is unique about Buddhist mantra.[48]

Buddhist mantra is not about shoring up or protecting one's sense of personal identity. Nor is it about feeling a sense of spiritual maturity or significance because one has a mantra to practise. Having a mantra bestowed upon you is not an affirmation of your spiritual development or a sign of progress. Mantra in a Buddhist context is about opening to and evoking specific enlightened qualities. There is an aspect of service and reverence in mantra. When we chant a mantra connected to a Buddhist figure of inspiration, we are not separate from the very 'being' or form that we are devoted to. Sangharakshita puts it best when he writes:

Bodhisattvas are within us potentially, just as the Enlightenment experience is within us potentially. When we repeat the mantras of Bodhisattvas, we are therefore in a way calling up our own inner forces, trying to get in touch with them [...] when we repeat the mantra of Avalokitesvara we are trying to make contact with our own innate compassion.[49]

We have the capacity for kindness and compassion to whatever degree, and so do others. Therefore, compassionate activity exists in the world as a potential – it is not personal compassion, but an innate presence of compassion in the world. When we authentically meet another's pain, know deeply that their experience of suffering is as valid as our own, our independent bodies are joined in compassion. Compassion is a bridge towards a stronger connection to our shared humanity. But more on that later. Let's return to mantra.

According to tradition, there are two main groupings of mantras – the informal and the formal. Informal mantras are performed outside of pujas and rituals, and are personal expressions of faith or confidence. They can be chanted internally or externally while going about one's daily life. Formal mantras may be handed down to you by a spiritual teacher to be repeated/recited within your own structured practice. These are also known as devotional mantras, and may find a central role in pujas and specific meditations. Their intention is to keep the Buddhist figure of devotion constantly in mind through the repetition of the mantra associated with that figure. Besides strengthening devotion, these mantras can become strong tools for focusing the mind. Moreover, through the practice of the mantra, the devotee has the potential to ignite insight.

Interestingly, a mantra is not necessarily a sound. Some argue that mantra is effective due to the 'vibrations' created within the body or between a group of people chanting the same mantra aloud. This may be true, and may give rise to strong experiences of connection and community, which can be valuable. But Sangharakshita makes it clear that a mantra is not an external or even an internal sound: a mantra is foremost a *symbol*. Mantras are key to a complex web of correlations, associations, traditions, and practices; they are not just the image of a Buddha or Bodhisattva transformed into sound. Thus, as a symbol, a mantra can be silent. Its visualized form, as much or in addition to its sound, has value if you have a deep realization of its meaning. And this is only gained through a long process of repetitions – 10,000 or 100,000 recitations are commonly cited. The practice of mantra offers the opportunity to bring the best in ourselves into relationship with the best in others and, more significantly, with aspects of the enlightened mind. This is achieved through sustained effort and receptivity.

In brief, if we refer to the four levels as a means of exploring mantra, we could say that:

- In *experiencing mantra*, we are encountering the sound, melody, forms, and colours of the syllables and investigating the internal response. Are we physically affected? Do we find certain emotional states or images arising? Do our confidence and faith feel energized? Are we inspired by the practice? Is there a shared sense of connection with others as we listen and engage with the sounds?

- When we move into *understanding mantra*, we begin to explore the meaning, if any, of the syllables and the various connections and associations they might have with specific figures from Buddhist cosmology. This study can inform and build upon our initial response.

- We begin *applying mantra* when we engage wholeheartedly with a mantra in a ritual context and in informal ways. This is particularly effective once one is given a mantra by a spiritual teacher (for instance at ordination into a Buddhist tradition). This becomes the touchstone of one's spiritual life, around which one's practice revolves.

- And, when *realizing mantra*, one becomes integrated with the skilful qualities and actions inherent in and associated with the mantra itself. The mantra becomes, as it were, one's spiritual heartbeat and way of acting in the world.

And so, now armed with an awareness of the purpose and practice of mantra, let's return to Avalokitesvara – the embodiment of compassion whose mantra is chanted at this juncture of the puja.

3. The sound of compassion

Here is the mantra written in Tibetan. It consists of six syllables, each characterized by a different colour and association. There are six colours, which correspond to the six classes of being according to Buddhist cosmology. One common representation of these beings and the six realms they inhabit is the bhavacakra, or wheel of becoming.

The wheel of becoming is a useful graphic reminder of the diversity of life. It can be easy to identify with one's own lived experience and lose sight of a wider perspective. All living beings exist in certain contexts and conditions. Some are blessed with ease and privilege; others endure abject poverty. Whole groups of people suffer dispossession and abuse, while others are blissfully unaware. We can live in our own world, our own bubble, and be ignorant of the plight of those around us. The wheel of becoming not only describes the conditions people live in, but also explains how each state came to be and how each being can be freed from their own special brand of discomfort. And, being a wheel, the fortunes of the individuals in each part are always in motion, transitioning from one state to another.

The realms are seen in the tradition as real locations (hell, heaven, etc.), but also as states of being in this world. Each of these six places or states of being has its own forms of suffering and dis-ease, yet hope exists in even the worst of places. In each of the realms, Avalokitesvara can be found working for the liberation of the inhabitants, illustrating how compassion is possible in every situation and between anyone. To chant Avalokitesvara's mantra is to wish and work for the liberation of each of these classes of beings. The mantra challenges us to consider the range of possible ways people experience life beyond the confines of our own existence. Its six colours refer to both the realms and the ways individuals can be freed from the constraints found there.

The six colours and syllables are also connected to the six paramitas or six perfections, which are a discrete path of practice for anyone aspiring to work for the benefit of all beings. The six perfecting practices – generosity, effort, ethics, patience, concentration, and wisdom – are represented as a means of liberating beings in all the realms of existence. You could think of the perfections as the actions taken as part of the imperative to remove suffering from individuals. First one meets the pain, and then one works to free those suffering.

Each syllable offers the beings in the corresponding realm what is needed to be free from the chains that bind them to suffering. Below you will see how each of the perfections can help those suffering in each of the realms.

The six colours of the mantra are:

- White: this is to liberate those who live in the heavenly realm of pleasure and indulgence. Traditionally, these beings are seen as gods or devas. Perhaps, these days, our gods are celebrities, social media influencers, our sports and movie stars. Chanting *om* purifies the lofty from their pride and arrogance. The white *om* is a fresh start (see Chapter 5). This syllable introduces those in the seemingly perfect world to the power and beauty of impermanence through the application of mindful attention. What the beautiful must see is the truth that this cannot last – this needs to be deeply appreciated. Thus, the perfection of concentration is needed.

- Green: this syllable frees those in the grip of jealous and avaricious thoughts. These are known as the asuras or titans, who are constantly driven to succeed at the expense of others. They are desperate to prove their superiority and fight all others in their way. Are these our contemporary crypto-currency traders or aggressive politicians? This syllable purifies the covetous with awareness of ethics and the consequences of actions. Are the titans aware of the people they trample over to get to the front of the queue? The perfection of ethics is needed for those who are desperate to prove themselves better than others.
- Yellow: this syllable is for those living in the everyday world that blends pleasure and pain in roughly equal measure. In other words: a normal human life. This is you on an average day. Human troubles are alleviated with a judicious application of endurance and distraction. Can we get through the next meeting, the next traffic jam, the latest Booker Prize winner, the next tedious blockbuster film, the friends' child's birthday party relatively unscathed? The perfection of patience is needed for those facing the average day.
- Turquoise: this syllable is for all animals and those driven by base instincts of survival and procreation. This could refer to actual animals, particularly those suffering in the world or imprisoned through unethical agricultural practices. Yet we can also live animalistic lives ourselves at times. We can get up, eat, leave the house, work, doze, and sleep with little or no awareness of how we got through each step in the day. This syllable offers an opportunity for those in this state to practise diligence and seek out a more elevated goal for life. The perfection of effort is needed.
- Red: this syllable is for those who are driven solely by greed, craving, and the sufferings of addiction. Traditional depictions of these 'hungry ghosts' show them as bloated beings with tiny mouths who are never satisfied. Besides people suffering from actual chemical addictions, we

can see people 'doom scrolling' through social media, obsessively building character stats in online games, or endlessly shopping online as being trapped in a spiral of addiction. Beings who crave experiences to feel the hit of 'I'm alive!' need to see the value and healing power of renunciation. To let go of the things that bind us is a great treasure. The perfection of generosity is needed for those who are burdened with craving.

- Dark blue: for those who suffer great torments, pain, and hatred, this syllable points to the great wisdom of the conditioned nature of existence. All phenomena are dependent upon conditions. Suffering does not just get doled out to us at the whim of a vindictive deity: suffering arises when certain conditions are in place. For example, eating heavily fried foods, leading a sedentary life, and not exercising, coupled with a genetic disposition for high blood pressure, can lead to the suffering of obesity and the pain of heart disease. This state of suffering is due to actions based on ignorance. In some cases, but not all, people suffer because of their own choices. For these people, the perfection of wisdom is needed.

Are we to be thinking of each of these realms and examples as we recite the mantra? Should we see the colours, the shapes of the letters? Yes and no. The shapes, colours, and associations are valuable to the extent that they open you up to being more compassionate in your life. Perhaps you have not considered the way we can create our own suffering, or have not contemplated that certain kinds of people, especially those with perfect skin, teeth, and abs, experience suffering. Allowing the mantra in, to resonate, to take root, is not like applying an encyclopedic knowledge of the meanings. They serve only to inform and challenge just who or what you believe deserving of compassion.

These six classes of being are part of our everyday experience – the angry driver, the distracted shop assistant, the confused elderly person ranting at the bus stop, the racist politician desperate for their point to be heard. All beings, even the inconvenient, irritating, and ignorant, suffer. Each one, regardless of our views about them, also has the capacity for Enlightenment. Yes, really. With this mantra you are saying, 'May they each find the way there suited to their situation.'

Take time to consider how you move through these states of being in a day, a week, a month, or a year. We can wake to a desperate need for coffee and the hopes that it will bring clarity to the day. Lurching to the gym, we may be driven by a jealous need to be fitter than the CrossFit influencer we follow on Instagram. We post a cheeky selfie, and check on the 'likes' during work meetings. By lunchtime, we have dealt skilfully with some challenging emails, and been cheered by some pleasant social interaction. Yet, as the afternoon approaches, our mind grows weary and our fantasy of a holiday on the beach takes hold. We may spend time scouring for options, and pop a few choice items (on sale of course with a promo code) into an online shopping cart. The commute home on the train could be a hellscape of delays, cancellations, overcrowded carriages, screaming babies, and body odour. We might lull ourselves into a pleasant sense of numbness with a drink, have a meal delivered by motor scooter by a student on a tenuous visa, and binge-watch episodes from a premium streaming service. This may not be an accurate depiction of your life (it may say more about me than you, to be honest), but there will be equivalents for you, and there will be for everyone. Which realms were you in today?

When we are in the presence of beings in the six realms (which is basically all the time), we have an opportunity to model the very qualities those beings need, qualities we need as well. When we apply the paramitas, we and those around us benefit. Consider being in the presence of friends who are obsessed with getting the latest upgrade to their lives, whether it is a home, job, or technological marvel. This is a perfect opportunity to explore ethical shopping and bring attention, in as non-puritanical a way as possible, to your own dilemmas of this kind. Consider being around those who are mired in anxiety and depression as an opportunity to share ways you have made yourself of service to others. The mantra alone will not liberate the world unless you also work for its liberation. And that's where we need Avalokitesvara.

4. 'The one who looks with compassion'

As mentioned above, Avalokitesvara is a non-historical figure, a figure of legend. They are depicted as luminous white, wearing regal attire and a crown adorned with a red jewel representing the infinite love of the Buddhas. The figure is identified as male, female, or neither depending on the tradition. Avalokitesvara's body is adorned with many accessories, suggesting the rich and precious nature of what they offer the world. But these are not the most unusual aspects. Avalokitesvara's four arms might strike you as the strangest feature.

We first encountered this figure in the puja through the sound of the mantra – *om mani padme hum* – although they appear twice more in the puja (in the *Heart Sutra*, which we will explore in a later chapter, and in the concluding mantras). Like most mantras or sacred syllables, the sounds mean very little in a literal sense. The closest translation would simply be 'purity jewel/stone lotus emptiness', which does little to clarify and doesn't do justice to the layers of meaning. Better to rest in the sound, let it resonate within and without, and see what arises. What do you notice after you have recited the mantra?

A clue to a possible reason for the placement of this mantra has something to do with the offerings verses that precede it in the Sevenfold Puja. In that verse, we welcome the honoured guest and reflect on what we might need to relinquish in order to proceed. This pre-empts a later verse called 'Confession of faults', but we'll come to that in due course. So now, at this point in the puja, we join our voices together in sounds intended to evoke universal compassion, for that is what Avalokitesvara stands for. As we bow and offer candles and incense, we realize that we are not only offering to the Buddha: now we are offering to all beings – all beings are the honoured guests.

All beings, according to the Buddha, are potentially Buddhas themselves. Everyone has the capacity to grow spiritually if the seeds are cultivated, seeds like the six perfections and other specific teachings. By evoking universal compassion, we are opening to this potential in ourselves and others. May everyone be free from suffering and become enlightened, that is my wish. We are beginning to move away from the personal to the interpersonal.

The image of Avalokitesvara and the mantra support this interpretation. Let's consider this through an examination of the image and just three of its many symbols – the mala, the lotus, and the jewel. Avalokitesvara holds a mala in the top right hand. A mala is used to count or record the recitation of mantras. Usually, it has 108 beads and is held in the right hand. It is an account of wholesome activity with body, speech, and mind (*om ah hum* again). The beads are counted through the movement of your fingers, your mind maintains focus on the words/meaning/effect, and your voice repeats the sound of the mantra. Thus, a mala is used to integrate these three parts of yourself – body, speech, and mind.

The mala is also a symbol of commitment to skilful acts through fealty and persistence. The mala has no beginning or end: it is a constant loop that to us is reminiscent of the mathematical symbol of infinity. Avalokitesvara's mala is made from pure crystal, suggesting that the one who wields the mala should act with the purest of intents and with a high degree of ethical sensitivity.

Crystal is a precious stone or jewel, and thus reminiscent of the *mani* in the mantra. It is solid, unyielding, clear, and radiant.

The lotus held in Avalokitesvara's top left hand (on the right of the image) is also associated with pristine ethics. A lotus is a flower that rises from mud and water before blooming untouched and unblemished. Thus, the lotus functions as a symbol of offering pure, ethical actions to others. This is also a symbol of the purified mind in meditation. The whiteness of the lotus again reinforces the understanding that, through actions, you are purified. This is the mind made beautiful through wholesome activity – the *padme* from the mantra. The lotus is soft, fragrant, and beautiful. It is symbolic of the fruits of a spiritual life.

Together we have crystal and lotus, stone and petal, practice and fruit of practice, effort and beauty, transformation and vision, activity and receptivity, masculine and feminine energies – the *mani* and the *padme*.

Avalokitesvara's other two arms are said to be holding the wish-fulfilling jewel close to the heart. This jewel, the chintamani, is no magical artefact, but a pictorial representation of a key concept or practice – bodhicitta. This is the wish for all beings to put aside that which holds them back, to cultivate that which is truly good, and to become fully and perfectly enlightened. The bodhicitta is also known as the heart of Awakening or the will to Enlightenment. This is the ultimate form of compassion – seeing the potential in others, and helping them to attain it and bring an end to suffering for themselves and all beings. The Sevenfold Puja is cited as being a main practice in the development of this attitude or will to work for the Enlightenment of all.

Avalokitesvara's four arms indicate that compassion reaches the four directions, but there are more than four directions mentioned even in the early texts. Ten or eleven directions are mentioned many times. Let's consider the arms in another way. What if the image of Avalokitesvara did not have four arms, but in effect only had two? What if we are seeing the image of him moving slowly through time? Two arms slowly coming together at the heart. Consider the wider two arms as him applying wholesome activity one moment at a time (the mala), and then offering up the fragrance of that action (the lotus) to others. Then we see them in the future. Imagine bringing those two together slowly, merging them, fusing them – ethical awareness merged with meditative appreciation. When you infuse them with an other-oriented attitude, you have the two hands at the heart offering Enlightenment to all.

Many people make the same hand gesture as in the image – the anjali or offering-lotus mudra – when chanting the mantra. By evoking Avalokitesvara with our hands, chanting the mantra, and setting our mind on universal compassion, we orient ourselves towards the next stage of the puja – 'Salutation'. Here the offering is magnified, if this is even possible:

> As many atoms as there are
> In the thousand million worlds,
> So many times I make reverent salutation
> To all the Buddhas of the Three Eras,
> To the Saddharma,
> And to the excellent Community.
>
> I pay homage to all the shrines,
> And places in which the Bodhisattvas have been.
> I make profound obeisance to the Teachers,
> And those to whom respectful salutation is due.

It is impossible to do what is stated here, at least literally. As many atoms as there are? Surely this is just hyperbole? Yes, the words are here to provide emphasis and energy, and underline a commitment. The lines evoke an aspiration or inclination to keep turning towards all that is good in the world. These words are suggestive of a relentless reverence, a constancy of devotion towards the Buddha as the exemplar, his teachings as a path, and the community that practises that path. Going for refuge, wanting to grow and develop, is not just a random thought or a curious pastime: it is a dynamic trajectory through life that requires intensity and consistency.

Moreover, we are opening to a wider Buddhist world in these verses. Our respect moves towards not only the historical Buddha, but the Buddhas of the past and the future too, indicating that

Enlightenment goes beyond time itself. That might be a bit much to take in at this point in the puja, but what it does point to is that, throughout time, there have been those who are wise guides who have transcended their limitations.

Again, it is hyperbole to say that one can worship at every shrine and every place in which a Bodhisattva has been. But you can recall uplifting places of beauty and inspiration that you have visited. They might not have a Buddha image or candles, but, in a sense, they are a shrine – a sacred space that moves one beyond the limits of the mundane. Also, you can remember moments of deep connection between individuals where one has helped the other to be free from what troubles them.

I often recall the profound sense of connection with others I experienced high on a ridgetop in the mountains of Spain. This lonely and jagged outcrop of limestone is a place I return to again and again in my mind. From this recollection, I derive great spiritual sustenance. As the sun set and a brisk warm breeze played with the hem of my robes, I knew that Enlightenment was more than a notion. Here I bowed with love for the world, though the wind threatened to dash me on the rocks below.

When we sense the pain of others, and are inspired by our deepest values to help, we can embrace both altruism and suffering. This is the liminal space where the essence of a Bodhisattva resides. And here, in these moments of kindness, we can bow to the possibility of change.

The verses contain some terms that may require some clarification. 'Buddhas of the Three Eras' refers to two key pieces of Buddhist thought. Firstly, that Enlightenment is timeless and not limited to those who had direct contact with the historical Buddha. Enlightenment is an attainable state that existed before Siddhartha Gautama, the historical Buddha. He rediscovered it, like an archeologist might discover the remains of a lost city. Secondly, the phrase refers to three specific figures – Dipankara, the Buddha of the past; Shakyamuni, the Buddha of the present; and Maitreya, the Buddha emerging in the future.

The 'Saddharma' is a name for the doctrine, teaching, religion, or path of practice. This is most often referred to as the Dharma (Sanskrit) or Dhamma (Pali). The Dharma is not just a book or series of texts.

It contains a much broader range of practices, approaches, and ways of living.

The 'excellent Community' is the sangha or fellowship of the Buddha's disciples. Early Buddhists and many traditions today consider the sangha to be those who have their commitment marked with an ordination – by joining a formal Buddhist order. Other traditions, such as the Triratna Buddhist Community, consider this term to apply more broadly to those who commit to practice, regardless of ordination. It is also important to understand that, when we repeat these verses, we are referring not only to those existing sangha members today but to all historical Buddhists, particularly those considered enlightened or inspiring teachers.

As we saw earlier in this chapter when referring to Avalokitesvara, a Bodhisattva is a being who works for the Enlightenment of others. Bodhisattvas are inspirations, and objects of devotion. Their qualities provide energy for one's life and practice.

5. Something to try

Looking back over this chapter can be daunting. After all, it is filled with layers and layers. Your mind might be swimming with information, and you might be left with the sense that you need to remember all this every time you chant and make offerings. Rest assured; you do not need to make all this conscious in every moment.

We have been building up our practice of Buddhist ritual over the past few chapters, starting with orienting our body, speech, and mind towards the Buddha, and then looking into the various offerings that we might make to confirm our commitment. Continue with the Threefold Puja as a regular practice. There might be an opportunity to perform it more times or less. You can decide.

You might like to add the Avalokitesvara mantra at the end of the final verse, and make offerings to the Three Jewels. In chanting the mantra, you'll note that the experience is quite different when it is just one person's voice. Nevertheless, it is a valuable practice to do.

Don't be overly concerned about getting the notes right, particularly if you are worried about not having a good singing voice. The purpose is to evoke compassion for yourself and the six ways in which beings experience life. Being critical of your vocal skill just erodes compassion.

Rest in the flow of the mantra as it weaves about you. May it help you understand and feel the truth that all beings, regardless of status, wealth, and education, experience dissatisfaction, discomfort, and even suffering, however mild or extreme. You do not need to be overwhelmed by this, for you do not bear the weight of it alone. After all, Avalokitesvara can lend a hand.

You could make offerings and bow to the shrine as you chant the *om mani padme hum* mantra. Remember, whatever offerings you make, the same has been offered and will be offered for millennia. You are not alone.

Also, see if you can make some time to reflect on the teaching of the six realms in a meaningful way. Who do you know in your direct experience who seems to live a life of ease and relative wellbeing? Perhaps everything they want and need seems to fall into their lap. This person leads a charmed life, like that of a god. You may know others who suffer from mental or physical ailments, and still others in the grips of addiction. How is your heart moved when you contemplate the lives of these individuals?

6. The chapter in review

- Everyone is united in experiencing discomfort, irritation, and suffering: what the Buddha called dukkha. This unites us, and so too does the wish to be free from suffering.

- Mantra is a way of contacting strong positive qualities within us for the benefit of all.
- The figure of Avalokitesvara embodies the urge to alleviate suffering through compassionate activity.
- Buddhist ritual practice invites us to look beyond ourselves to the sufferings of others in whatever way their lives manifest.
- We are not alone in this good work. There are those who have trodden the same paths as us through history, and those presently walking by our side.

Chapter Eight

Refuge: Where Is Safety in the World?

To many places beings withdraw
to escape from fear:
to mountains, forests,
parklands and gardens;
sacred places as well.
But none of these places
offer true refuge,
none of them can free us from fear.

One who finds refuge in the Buddha
in the Dhamma and in the Sangha
sees with penetrating insight:
suffering, its cause, its release
and the Way leading to true freedom.

The Buddha, the Dhamma, the Sangha:
these are the true refuge;
these are supreme;
these lead to Liberation.

> *Dhammapada* verses on the Buddha, translated by
> Ajahn Munindo[50]

1. Going for refuge: an island of safety

In Australia, as in many countries, traffic can be extremely dangerous
and even hazardous to your health. Though the risk of injury isn't

as high as in some parts of India, the traffic in Australian cities is not to be underestimated. This is perhaps why good city planners create 'traffic islands' – small places of calm amidst the raucous to-ing and fro-ing of cars, trucks, and taxis. They provide a bare minimum of security in a difficult situation.

Traffic islands are a useful metaphor for the ways in which we seek solace, safety, and security amongst the chaos of life. These 'islands' take many forms. Our hobbies and interests can be temporary circuit breakers from the daily stressors of working life. Career, popularity, and success can also seem to give us what we seek, but for many there remain existential questions not answered by pay cheques, fame, or awards.

The views we hold can be seductive too, but, as we know already, views are changeable and dependent on circumstances. A true refuge, according to Buddhists, is one that is not dependent, that is not reliant upon other things being in place. A true place of safety is one that can be accessed regardless of the time, situation, price tag, or special equipment. It is not dependent on 10,000 Buddha statues or wooden fish. A true and reliable refuge is thus always present if one has the inclination to look for it. A true refuge leads one away from suffering. Thus, a refuge is not a place, or a person, or a group, but an attitude or inclination that leads one towards freedom.

You might argue, however, that a shrine, offerings, and Dharma books are conditions upon which our practice is dependent. Do we not need a centre to attend, candles to light, and incense to burn? No. No we don't. These are useful conditioning factors in that they can help curiosity and devotion to develop, but do not mistake the vehicle for the journey. The Buddha had none of these things to become enlightened, only his practice. You can meditate anywhere and at any time. Right now, even. You can be kind anywhere and at any time. You can perform puja at any place and at any time. If your practice is dependent upon external objects and forms, then you are limiting the potential of the practice by clinging to the fetter of habit.

A true refuge is present when the heart and mind turn towards liberation, the path, and the inspiration of those who have walked it – in other words, the Three Jewels. This going for refuge is not reliant upon objects or artefacts, or even language. Going for refuge can be a silent voice, a yearning voice that speaks no words but communicates with the language of the heart.

It may seem counter to everything we've explored above – all the symbols and objects and items – but it is a priority to look beyond those and search for the silent voice that has devotion for the Buddha, the Dharma, and the Sangha. That voice is the one worth listening to. It is of greater value than the expensive Buddha statues and imported Japanese incense you offer.

2. Going for refuge back in the Buddha's time

When people encountered the Buddha face to face some 2,600 years ago, it was often a life-changing experience. They came to the Buddha with questions and concerns that are not all that unlike our own: questions about how to remove difficulties and experience true freedom. Though the languages, technologies, and political models have changed since the fifth century BCE, human frailties, passions, drives, and dreams have not changed one iota.

When people met the Buddha, they were not always respectful or even 'sold' on him as an enlightened being, as we saw with Bharadvaja the haughty Brahmin. Many who presented themselves were highly critical of the Buddha and his growing movement of wandering ascetics. They questioned and even condemned his methods, much as some might today see Buddhism as selfish navel gazing. Others, of course, came to him feeling profoundly reverential, and demonstrated their respect wholeheartedly. Regardless of the initial attitude they held, almost everyone left his presence changed in some way. For some, Enlightenment was immediately attained. For others, a clear path of practice was laid out, for which they felt deep and abiding gratitude.

The Pali canon records the Buddha's interactions with his many visitors over his forty years of teaching. The stories often follow a similar pattern:

1. The setting is established: the location of the meeting is described, including a list of the main participants in the tale.

2. A lay person, a monk, a member of a royal house, or even a deity approaches the Buddha with a question or a dilemma.
3. The Buddha asks questions skilfully to help the person understand what the causes of the problem are. Dialogue between the Buddha and the questioner ensues.
4. The Buddha might then tell a story or provide a detailed analysis of the causes and conditions involved. He might also suggest specific practices or frameworks that would address the issues inherent in the person's question.
5. There might be a poetic rendering of the same teaching at the end, or interspersed throughout.
6. The listener/questioner has their eyes opened. They have a eureka or lightbulb moment, and profess their admiration, respect, gratitude, and thanks to the Buddha.

This final point is recorded in the original texts quite simply, but later texts create a common refrain or formula that captures, in a poetic sense, the enormity of the impact the meeting has had. Here is one version of the refrain.

Excellent, Lord, excellent! It is as if someone were to set up what had been knocked down, or to point out the way to one who had got lost, or to bring an oil-lamp into a dark place, so that those with eyes could see what was there. Just so the Blessed Lord has expounded the Dhamma in various ways. And I, Lord, go for refuge to the Blessed Lord, to the Dhamma, and to the Sangha.[51]

The images here are clear. The Buddha's teaching puts things right, provides direction, and illuminates the dark places. This is what inspires people to make the personal choice to 'go for refuge'. Some want a solution to the challenges they face – their lives need to be 'picked up'. Others feel directionless, and are searching for a purpose – they need the way to be pointed out. Others are driven by a need to understand and to feel hope – they seek a light in the shadows. Have you had a moment like this in your spiritual journey?

There is a beautiful and more simple exaltation of going for refuge in a short verse in the *Therigatha*, which is a collection of poems written by early Buddhist nuns. This piece, entitled 'Punnika and the Brahman', recounts a conversation between the nun and a traditional Vedic practitioner who asserts that one needs to bathe in water to free oneself from past evil deeds. This is reminiscent of the Brahminic practice we encountered earlier with the surly Brahmin Bharadvaja. In this situation, the nun Punnika sets the man straight on how one is really freed:

> If you're afraid of pain,
> if you dislike pain,
> go to the Awakened One for refuge,
> go to the Dhamma & Sangha.
> Take on the precepts:
> That will lead to your liberation.[52]

3. Refuges and precepts

Today, the most frequently repeated verses of going for refuge are these:

> *Buddham saranam gacchami*
>   To the Buddha for refuge I go
> *Dhammam saranam gacchami*
>   To the Dhamma for refuge I go
> *Sangham saranam gacchami*
>   To the Sangha for refuge I go

These three lines are repeated three times during the refuge ceremony, which marks the act of becoming or reaffirming oneself as a Buddhist. They are said a second and a third time to indicate the importance of the refuge in one's life. The first time may be said to publicly acknowledge that one is a Buddhist. The second time to indicate to oneself that one is truly committed, and thirdly to set oneself firmly on the path for the liberation of all beings.

Reciting the words places one in a tradition of practice that goes back thousands of years. To say the words in call and response is to echo the lives of the billions of Buddhists who preceded you and those who are yet to arise. We are part of a continuity of practice. Again, this is a common theme in this ritual.

The refuges are traditionally followed by the five precepts for lay people and those who are not ordained. Once we join the Triratna Buddhist Order, we recite ten precepts, though only in the company of other Order members. Other traditions have their own formulations of precepts or rules for practitioners.

Precepts are curious things that can be misinterpreted, particularly if one has a Judaeo-Christian background. Precepts are not rules or commandments that one promises to keep for fear of judgement. Instead, they are trainings or practices we decide to take on and to test. Reciting them is a reminder to bear them in mind; chanting them together in puja it is a collective reminder of our shared values.

In applying the precepts, we honour the refuges and draw closer to what they embody through emulation. Basically, we turn to the Three Jewels out of respect and reverence, then we move towards them through our actions of body, speech, and mind by practising the precepts. As well as moving towards the Three Jewels, we also move them into the centre of our mind and heart.

Sangharakshita makes the connection between going for refuge and the precepts clear when he writes in *The Ten Pillars*:

> The placing of the Buddha at the centre of one's
> personal mandala corresponds to Going for Refuge. The
> radical reorganisation of the contents of that mandala
> corresponds to the observance of the Precepts as its natural
> consequence, that is to say, as the prolongation of the
> act of Going for Refuge itself into every aspect of one's
> existence.[53]

Thus, as you devote yourself more and more to the ideal, you act more and more in accord with the ideal, transforming into a Dharma being, a Bodhisattva if you will. To take this further, to become a Bodhisattva, you need to train and learn the skills of the trade. To be someone who acts for the welfare of others, start acting for the welfare of others.

The practice of the precepts begins with an intention to try them out and observe the results, as a goldsmith might test gold in a crucible to discern the carats. By refining yourself through ethical practice, you remove negative habits and replace them with more wholesome ways.

Let's revisit the four levels in the context of ethics. We'll start with the body and the bodily actions in which we engage – both the skilful and the unskilful – before moving on to actions of speech and of mind. The focus here will be on the five precepts.

Body precepts – *om*

> Pali – *Panatipata veramani-sikkhapadam samadiyami*
> Translation – I undertake to abstain from taking life.
> Positive practice – With deeds of loving kindness, I purify my
>   body.

If we can refrain from causing harm to living beings though our bodily actions with our *experience* and reflect on the impacts of such actions, we can come to a deeper *understanding* of how all beings, including ourselves and those we dislike, wish to live lives unhindered by pain or cruelty. This is a universal truth. In addition, we can grow to appreciate the talents and skills of ourselves and others and, by *applying* ourselves wholeheartedly to goodwill, we will come closer to *realizing* a state of constant, kind awareness that sees all beings as they truly are, undistorted by views.

> Pali – *Adinnadana veramani-sikkhapadam samadiyami*
> Translation – I undertake to abstain from taking the not-given.
> Positive practice – With open-handed generosity, I purify my
>   body.

If we only take that which is freely given to us, rather than constantly acquiring or taking things by force, we come to appreciate the unique beauty of the resources the world offers us. We can experience a sense of abundance and a wish to share that abundance with others. In this way, we move from a miserly world view to one motivated by generosity. By applying ourselves to sharing our material goods, our time, and the Dharma, we can gain an even greater appreciation of others and their talents as we help provide them with what they need. Giving supports connection when it is done without need for reciprocation. Applying ourselves to providing for others reveals a great wisdom – nothing is truly owned except for the consequences of one's actions. Thus we can make space in our lives for what really matters and afford others the same opportunity. To realize the great insight of generosity is to see all beings and every moment as an opportunity to celebrate and share unconditionally.

Pali – *Kamesu micchacara veramani-sikkhapadam samadiyami*
Translation – I undertake to abstain from sensual/sexual misconduct.
Positive practice – With stillness, simplicity, and contentment, I purify my body.

We can experience great pleasure and joy from and with our bodies, whether that be from exercise or food or sexual encounters. This ethical precept asks us not to avoid or remove all sensual experiences, but to refrain from those that potentially cause harm, either through over-indulgence or through the use of power to get what we want from others. Whether an act is considered misconduct or not depends on the motivating factors, not necessarily the act itself. Exploring our motives is how we come to a deeper understanding of the place of contentment in the spiritual life. We are invited to move inwards and become less reliant upon the external world to provide us with a sense of fulfilment or gratification. We begin to apply this in our everyday life by seeing the limitations of sensual delights, and choose to move away from them. In turn, we can even come to appreciate how craving pleasure is the root of suffering. Fully realizing this state is to live free from covetousness and avarice. We live a life of deep contentment.

Speech precepts – *ah*

Pali – *Musavada veramani-sikkhapadam samadiyami*
Translation – I undertake to abstain from false speech.
Positive practice – With truthful communication, I purify my speech.

Approaching Enlightenment

Words can be used to construct generous, kind, and clear environments in which no one is afraid or uneasy. Words feed into perceptions, judgements, and subjective realities. Speaking truthfully and with compassion, one can create clarity for oneself and others. Untruths, however, construct reality in one-sided ways, and are most often tinged with self-interest, ill-will, fear, and/or confusion. We can exaggerate in order to garner a specific response from the listener. We might falsify records to try and avoid unpleasant consequences or to gain a undeserved reward. In making untrue statements, we seek to bend external conditions to our will to match the view we hold of ourselves as someone more deserving than others. This is self-clinging at its most self-preserving.

By coming to understand our reasons for constructing untruths, we can begin to reflect on the impacts such actions have on others, our reputation, and ourselves. Such behaviour shapes a world in which we must protect ourselves and deceive others to maintain an illusion. But this goes even further when we consider the ways in which self-talk can be infused with untruths. We can forge unhelpful narratives and identities that raise us up or tear us down. Such internal words create worlds of pain for us, and impact heavily on how we engage with the world. Understanding this, we must apply ourselves to the truth, even if it is painful or inconvenient, and even if it points us towards areas of ourselves that must be changed. Realizing this practice, we can speak our truths in kindly, non-malicious, helpful, and harmonious ways.

Mind precepts – *hum*

Pali – *Surameraya majja pamadatthana veramani-sikkhapadam samadiyami*
Translation – I undertake to abstain from taking intoxicants.
Positive practice – With mindfulness clear and radiant, I purify my mind.

These days, a huge number of intoxicants are on offer. Obviously, alcohol, sex, and drugs remain temptations to help us bear reality or try and escape it entirely, but there are far more insidious ones than these. We can be intoxicated by opinions and views, particularly those espoused publicly and prolifically on social media. Our minds can become clouded and obscured by shopping for the best and latest items, as we think in our delusion that such objects can provide us with some degree of lasting happiness. Understanding that we might have an addictive tendency and shining a light on it are the first steps towards wisdom. If we can illuminate our habits and our motives with a compassionate attitude, we have the possibility of freeing ourselves. Thus, by becoming aware of the impact certain elements have on our internal life and how that plays out in our lived experience, we can start to unravel the conditions that we are bound to. This is done through a consistent, persistent, and patient application of mindfulness. If mindful attention is applied to all aspects of our lives, in much the same way as the sun shines on all things evenly, the obscuring darkness of intoxication and ignorance can be dispelled.

Ethics, when actively practised, has the potential to connect us deeply to the positive aspects of our shared humanity – kindness, generosity, contentment, truthfulness, and mindfulness. When these are refined and fully realized, we draw closer to Buddhahood.

4. The 'rounds of rebirth'

Within a puja, there will be verses such as the one that follows. This is taken from the Sevenfold Puja:

> This very day
> I go for my refuge
> To the powerful protectors,
> Whose purpose is to guard the universe;
> The mighty conquerors who overcome suffering
> everywhere.
>
> Wholeheartedly also I take my refuge
> In the Dharma they have ascertained,
> Which is the abode of security against the rounds of rebirth.
> Likewise in the host of Bodhisattvas
> I take my refuge.

The 'powerful protectors' or conquerors referred to here are other enlightened beings, such as Avalokitesvara, whom we met earlier, and a series of other non-historical Buddhas known as the jinas or conquerors.[54]

There are phrases in these going for refuge verses that need some unpacking. The 'abode of security' refers to the nature of the Dharma as a refuge – a safe place, just like the traffic island, but much more secure. The 'rounds of rebirth' will require more careful consideration.

There are two main ways of addressing 'rebirth': through your direct experience, and through, well, faith. Let's begin with experience – are you the same person you were when you were seven years old? You retain some memories perhaps, and even some characteristics both physical and psychological, but they are weak compared to the person you are today. Back then your chief concerns may have been substantially different from those of today. Even your physical body has grown, replenished itself, and changed size. (Did you know that your body's cells are completely changed over seven years?) You have consumed matter, deposited matter, integrated ideas, and changed ideas innumerable times. Habits have come and gone. Interests have come and gone. Moods, fashion choices, bad hair days. There have been days of tears, of incandescent rage, of laughter, and flowing ease. There have been days you have been desperate to see come to an end, and others you have wished would last forever. In other words, you have lived many, many lives within the confines of this round of embodied existence.

The Buddhist tradition can address rebirth in a variety of ways. In a text known as the *Sutra of Forty-Two Sections* (translated into Chinese in the Ming Dynasty),[55] there is some discussion about the length of a human life. How long does a person live? After some put forward the standard amounts – the equivalent of four score and ten – the Buddha says that the length of a human life is only one breath. One breath. In-breath – arising. Out-breath – passing away. Think about that for a moment. Who are we in that breath? What is alive in you for the duration of that breath? What are the qualities of this precious moment of being alive? What is met, understood, and released in that cycle of breathing? String individual breaths together, and you have a whole rosary of breaths, a round of rebirths reminiscent of Avalokitesvara's crystal mala. Are your breaths, is your life, as crystal clear?

And then we have the teaching of the six realms of existence, which we explored in Chapter 7. These are presented as being in a wheel – an actual 'round' shape that we cycle or spiral around. Avalokitesvara brings a compassionate heart to each of the six realms, offering just what is needed in each to bring the denizens to liberation, or at the very least to alleviate their unique suffering. Each syllable of the mantra calls out to free beings. Each syllable resonates with perfecting energies that target specific needs.

Remember that beings in the realm of the gods have everything their hearts desire, but no wider awareness outside of personal pleasure. They need to learn how to see themselves and the world more widely, hence Avalokitesvara (or compassion) teaches god-like affluent beings how to concentrate and focus the mind in order to see the truth. This is not further self-indulgence, but the capacity to see the truth and let go. Those who are driven by intense jealousy are, through compassion, instructed to reflect on the consequences of their actions. The addicted are encouraged to give to others. Those in pain and torment are asked to reflect on the conditions that give rise to suffering. Beings whose lives are limited to meeting animal cravings are asked to lift themselves up with sustained effort, and those who live a blend of all the above are reminded to be patient with all that comes.

The Buddhist tradition is clear that such realms exist, and not just in a psychological sense – though that might be easier for us to connect with. We can experience intense suffering, intense desire, and overwhelming jealousy. We can be reborn into these states from one breath to the next, yet do we believe that the entity we call 'me' will die and migrate to another such form?

This is not the place to investigate what is reborn if there is no soul – a classic question for Buddhists. Instead, let your experience or ritual dictate your actions.[56]

5. Something to try

To strengthen your practice and to build in more aspects of compassion and ethics, continue with the practice of the Threefold Puja, but consider adding some elements, such as the lines below.

Here is the structure of a typical session. This could take as little as ten minutes, or last as long as you want.

1. Opening reverence

2. Reverence to the Three Jewels, followed by refuges and precepts in Pali, and positive precepts in English.

Buddham saranam gacchami
Dhammam saranam gacchami
Sangham saranam gacchami
Dutiyampi buddham saranam gacchami
Dutiyampi dhammam saranam gacchami
Dutiyampi sangham saranam gacchami
Tatiyampi buddham saranam gacchami
Tatiyampi dhammam saranam gacchami
Tatiyampi sangham saranam gacchami
Panatipata veramani-sikkhapadam samadiyami
Adinnadana veramani-sikkhapadam samadiyami
Kamesu micchacara veramani-sikkhapadam samadiyami
Musavada veramani-sikkhapadam samadiyami
Surameraya majja pamadatthana veramani-sikkhapadam samadiyami
Sadhu sadhu sadhu

With deeds of loving kindness, I purify my body.
With open-handed generosity, I purify my body.
With stillness, simplicity, and contentment, I purify my body.
With truthful communication, I purify my speech.
With mindfulness clear and radiant, I purify my mind.

3. Offerings to the Buddha

Avalokitesvara mantra and offerings[57]

Something else to consider is establishing an ethical practice, including preparation and reflection. Here are some questions you could reflect on:

- How might you bring attention to the Three Jewels throughout the day?
- How do you intend to practise loving kindness towards yourself and others?
- How will you be generous and celebrate the beauty of life?
- How will you invest in silence, contentment, and ease?
- How will you shape your words to create a space of honesty, unity, and courage?
- How will you cultivate a quieter and more focused mind?

6. The chapter in review

- A true state of safety in the world relies on a constant turning towards your highest ideals. For a Buddhist, this is the Three Jewels – the Buddha, the Dharma, and the Sangha.
- Going for refuge is a stage of Buddhist ritual, but it is more than that: it is an inclination or direction, and an activity.
- Going for refuge can be a powerful outpouring of faith and devotion.
- Encountering the Dharma can have a profound impact on how you live the rest of your life.
- Engaging with the precepts brings you closer to the qualities they represent.
- A life aligned with Buddhist ethics can provide support and inspiration.
- The six realms of existence are, on one level, an illustration of the ways in which suffering can manifest. Compassion is a remedy that can take many forms.
- We are reborn in every moment, perhaps with every breath.

Approaching Enlightenment

Chapter Nine

Confession: How Can I Be Better?

There is no cosmic policeman handing out speeding tickets.
It is our own actions that help create our character.

Sangharakshita, *Living Ethically*[58]

1. Confession of faults: the face of evil

The previous stage of the puja asks us to commit to an ethical path through recitation of the precepts. This new phase of the practice encourages us to make an honest appraisal of our ethical life: do our actions live up to our aspirations? Here is the text from the 'Confession of faults' section of the Sevenfold Puja:

The evil that I have heaped up
Through my ignorance and foolishness –
Evil in the world of everyday experience,
As well as evil in understanding and intelligence –
All that I acknowledge to the Protectors.

Standing before them
With hands raised in reverence,
And terrified of suffering,
I pay salutations again and again.

May the Leaders receive this kindly,
Just as it is, with its many faults!
What is not good, O Protectors,
I shall not do again.

Evil. The word jumps out to the modern reader. For some, the word 'evil' is problematic or even triggering. Evil may be an accusation levelled against your actions or even against you as a person. Good and evil can be unhelpful binary notions that oversimplify complex situations. In some world views, evil is a thing, a noun, a characteristic possessed by certain types of people. In this view, evil must be atoned for, or it will find release into the world through actions. This is *not* how this word is being applied here in this verse.

So what *is* evil in a Buddhist sense?

Let me tell you that evil does exist. You can come face to face with a true embodiment of evil that may chill you to the bone. I had to go to Kathmandu to see it, but you may not need to go so far.

One of the holiest places on the planet is Boudhanath – a short, bumpy taxi ride from Nepal's capital. There, surrounded by temples and shops, is an astonishing construction called the Buddha Stupa. Its enormous, white-washed dome and golden spire have survived earthquakes and coups. It is also a UNESCO world heritage site. The enormous Buddha eyes near the top look unblinkingly across the Kathmandu valley. All beings are encompassed in that compassionate gaze.

If you enter one of the more elaborate temple porticos, you see abandoned sandals and a thick blanket of incense smoke. Ascending stairs take you into a semi-darkened space hung with multicoloured brocades and lit with spluttering lamps. Long red benches face inwards. Golden statues peer out benevolently from the shadows. But, if you turn around, behind you on the wall is a frightening mural that stops you in your tracks.

The figure is about four metres tall and a deep blue, almost black. Its bloated six-armed form is wreathed in layers of flame. A shred of tiger skin is tucked about its nether regions. Beneath its feet are what appear to be naked human beings crying out for help. Each of its six hands has vicious claws that wield strange items. Its fangs are bared in a maniacal laugh. Its three eyes bulge out, staring down, but not quite at you. You are dwarfed by this terrifying vision. This is Mahakala, the Great Black One. Mahakala is a figure common to both Hindus and Tibetan Buddhists. If you

spend time taking it in, the creature almost seems to be moving, dancing even. Here is evil, taunting you.

As you might imagine, early Christian missionaries to Nepal and Tibet saw images like this and thought Buddhism to be a hive of demons. They were completely wrong, and they should have known better. For centuries, gargoyles have clung tenaciously to the cathedrals of Europe, with the purpose of scaring evil away. So too jack-o'-lanterns glare out from doorsteps at Hallowe'en. Mahakala functions in much the same way, by scaring you into remembering your vows and your practice. But how?

It is important when we first encounter the presence or image of Mahakala that we do not launch into trying to analyze and understand the figure on a purely intellectual level, with a false sense of security. To fully experience the image, we must feel the response, the discomfort, and even the revulsion. You might feel the reverse of this: the image may excite you, spur you into action and enquiry.

For the majority, the image of Mahakala is not attractive or gentle or overtly kind, but neither are our unskilful habits and actions. When we look deeply, do we experience remorse, regret, and fear of censure from those we admire? Mahakala is asking us to feel into the fear, and see that its horrible, misshapen form is who we might become if we continue to act contrary to our values, our precepts.

You could think of Mahakala as our own version of the picture of Dorian Gray. In Oscar Wilde's novel, the narcissist Dorian sits to have a portrait painted of himself in the prime of his youth. During the sitting, Dorian expresses something that has terrifying consequences:

> He had uttered a mad wish that he himself might remain young, and the portrait grow old; that his own beauty might be untarnished, and the face on the canvas bear the burden of his passions and his sins; that the painted image might be seared with the lines of suffering and thought.[59]

Mr Gray lives his life without regard for others, focusing on his own gratification and pleasure. While he remains young and vigorous, the painting – hidden in the attic – bears the scars of his egregious choices. Whereas Dorian cannot bear to look upon the painting for fear of seeing the terrible consequences of his actions, here in the image of Mahakala and in this verse of the puja, we are asked to summon the courage to peek.

Mahakala is a reminder of the urgency to practise in this very life, for it is short and filled with terrors. His hideous form reminds us of our own failings, our own dereliction of the practice. It says: wake up! Time is short! Get on with what you promised! Your ego and desire for pleasure squirm beneath the feet of the beast.

This is confronting, and necessarily so. Mahakala is the other side of the compassion coin. Whereas Avalokitesvara looks down on beings with a deep abiding compassion, Mahakala, the dark twin, is kicking us up the backside and rubbing our face in our own mess. The Great Black One and the One Who Looks Upon Us with Compassion are reflexive forms of the same practice of universal compassion.

Mahakala's six arms are a visual reminder to practise the six perfections that we have already discussed when examining Avalokitesvara – the practices of giving, ethics, patience, effort, concentration, and wisdom. The objects he wields in those arms are to help us cut the chains that bind us, reminding us of our intentions and rousing us back onto the path we have strayed from. Let's try and understand these tools, so that we may apply them in our practice.

In one of his right hands is a chopper, not to inflict physical harm but to sever attachments to those things that hold us back – habits, views, possessions. On the corresponding left is a bowl made from a human skull. This can be seen as a visceral reminder to offer everything that one does and is to living beings. One of the upper arms carries a mala, like the one carried by Avalokitesvara. Here the crystal beads are replaced by grinning skulls – are we allowing our unwholesome habits to die moment by moment? The corresponding hand holds a trident, honed to strike at the heart of our greed, ill-will, and delusion. The lower arms wield a drum and a lasso. The former is to rouse us into action, to dance to the beat of the Dharma, and the latter is to catch us in that moment before we succumb to our negative habits.

Objects held by Mahakala	Corresponding perfection
Chod knife – chopper	Wisdom (*prajna*) The severing of all views and unhelpful conceptions
Kapala – a bowl made from the top of a human skull	Generosity (*dana*) Offering up everything from the beautiful to the ugly
Mala – skull rosary	Patience (*kshanti*) Being present to each moment, even the painful ones, and letting go
Trishula – trident	Ethics (*sila*) Piercing craving, aversion, and ignorance at the root
Damaru – drum	Effort (*virya*) Rousing energy and joy
Pasha – lasso	Concentration (*samadhi*) Connecting and unifying attention

Since that encounter in a temple in Kathmandu, I have often wondered to what extent I avoid looking at myself and my actions. Does fear of seeing the worst in me stop me changing? On the flipside, do I also refuse to see skilful acts and qualities I embody? Basically, am I just afraid to see both sides of me and the grey areas in between?

So, in the 'Confession of faults' verses in a puja, sometimes called the declaration, we are invited to look at ourselves honestly and fearlessly, and say with confidence, 'No, not on my watch. Not anymore.'

2. Actions and consequences

Dorian Gray felt himself immune to the consequences of his actions – the painting took all of that on itself and bore the horrendous scars. For those of us much wiser, and less fictional, we know the truth. One does not need to be a Buddhist to understand the truth that actions have consequences. Sometimes this is how the Buddhist teachings around karma are explained. This is a limited definition, though far from the most misleading.

Karma is not, despite much popular writing on the subject, about 'what goes around comes around'. That erroneous view holds that good things come to those who do good and, conversely, the sinful will ultimately suffer. It takes but a minute to see the error of this. People you know who are kindly and generous fall victim to debilitating illnesses. Those who manipulate others out of a desire for attention and power get elected to political office. Karma is not so black and white.

Karma means 'action'. We know already that we act with our bodies, our speech, and even our minds. These actions leave marks on us, others, and the world. If I start doing push-ups every day and commit to building a habit, they will get easier in time and I will reap the health and aesthetic benefits. But situations are rarely as simple or as easy to determine in real life.

Given at the right time, a friendly smile directed at someone who is struggling can brighten the day for both parties. The same smile at the wrong time could be experienced as condescending, whatever the intention. This can pull apart two people who need connection. You might have the intention to be kind, but other factors can confuse the message. This can also cause individuals to consider whether such kindly actions are advisable in the future.

There is a myriad of conditions at play whenever we act – history, culture, psychology, biology, agency, spirituality... Take subcultures or groups that we may participate in, for example. In some groups, acts of kindness and generosity are actively derided in favour of world-weary cynicism. In other narcissistic ventures, cruelty and selfishness are celebrated. And still in others, selfless giving is cherished more than self-care. How we choose to act in these groups and societies can feel constrained and limited. We may feel pressured into conformity or even lose the hope that we can make long-lasting change, but the truth is we can – we may not reap the benefits ourselves, but those who follow in our footsteps will.

Karma is not a condemnation but a calling to embrace change, one action at a time. If we are proponents of Enlightenment and wish for all to be free from suffering, it is important to consider to what extent our actions are in accord with our aspirations. This section of the puja is drawing our attention in this direction.

The 'Confession of faults' verse in the puja asks us to look at our lives honestly and openly, without hiding away the less appealing aspects. We might not think of them as 'evil' per se, but they are in opposition to the more refined goals to which we aspire. How does an inner monologue of judgement align with the wish for all beings to be happy? How does taking up all the talking space in a study group match up with the practice of open-handed generosity?

We are being asked to take stock of our actions, not to punish ourselves for 'not being good enough' – that is more akin to guilt, which spirals away and gnaws at our capacity for agency. These verses are not about guilt – they are asking us to actively consider the impacts we have made. Remorse or shame – feeling the difficult, uncomfortable truth of our misdeeds, unpleasant as it is – is listed by the Buddha as a positive mental state. Remorse is a launching point for a deeper skilfulness. But to get to that more purified state, we need to know exactly what we have done and be convinced that it is not in line with our higher purpose.

What makes an act unwholesome? If an action is motivated by

greed, aversion, or ignorance, it is bound to lead to suffering for oneself, others, and the world at some point. Conversely, an action that is motivated by generosity, loving kindness, and clarity will lead to more positive states. The fruits of these actions might not arise immediately; as mentioned above, there are many, many other conditions to consider in any given situation, but the karma will ripen in due course. The consequences of kindness and of cruelty will eventually be experienced in this life or in ones to come.

Once we see what we have done clearly and tenderly, then kindness and putting to rights are the medicine we need. The energy of Mahakala may be the wake-up call to pull us back, remind us of our purpose, and get to work, but it is Avalokitesvara's unyielding compassion that supports us along the way and provides what we need. We can be both aspects for ourselves, to ourselves, and perhaps even for others.

'Confession of faults' verses are not about punishing ourselves and wallowing in 'wickedness'; no, we are facing up to and moving on. This is the act of confession – communicating what we have done and how we intend to act from this moment.

But this begs the question, to whom do we confess?

3. Confession

It is often said that, according to Buddhism, you can only save yourself. The *Dhammapada*, a very early collection of sayings of the Buddha, states unequivocally that it is all up to us:

> By ourselves we do evil
> and by ourselves we are made impure.
> By ourselves we avoid evil
> and by ourselves we are made pure.
> The matter of purity is our own affair.
> No other can be responsible.[60]

We are the prime movers, this verse states. We are the creators and destroyers, not other beings. Not God. Not the Buddha. Not Avalokitesvara. So how do we reconcile this with the words we recite here? How does acknowledging our shortcomings to the protectors work?

We've established that there are forces at work in the universe that we clothe in forms to which we can more easily relate. These beings embody such liberating ideals as universal compassion. Over millennia, complex associations, names, and correspondences have been developed through reflection and meditation on these powers at work.

So, when we speak of the 'powerful protectors' and us 'standing before them with hands raised in reverence, and terrified of suffering', just what are we asking these beings to be? Are we to think of them as Buddhist saints or deities who can intercede on our behalf and whisk away our wrongdoings with a few 'hail Avalokitesvaras'? Will saying a few *om mani padme hums* absolve us from sin?

No. And Yes.

No, we are the ones who have acted unskilfully and who must make amends. You have shouted angrily at your partner, and that cannot be taken back. You collected the organic onions and put in the much cheaper price for the regular ones at the self-serve checkout. You have secretly texted someone behind your partner's back, knowing that it's wrong but enjoying it nevertheless. Exaggerating the misery of a family visit to garner sympathy from co-workers isn't lying, is it? This action cannot be undone or taken back, but we can work to not commit such acts again.

In the verses, we call on the protectors to witness our unskilful actions, but also to witness that we will commit to not doing them again. We are opening ourselves up, becoming vulnerable and honest, not just to ourselves but to the forces in the universe that we hold to be the highest. Having gone for refuge, we have placed our heart and mind on the Buddha, his teaching, and the community of practitioners; we fall short and must dispense with what holds us back. We call on them to witness and support us in making more informed choices in the future. Will wisdom still our tongue? Will compassion help us see what motivates our behaviour?

No, the protectors cannot save us... unless, of course, they can. There are many practices in the Buddhist tradition that suggest that the protectors can be called upon to act as supports. There are innumerable prayers and pujas dedicated to Buddhas and Bodhisattvas that request intervention. Sadhana practices, sometimes called visualization practices, encourage the practitioner to visualize light entering the body and dissolving negative tendencies and past unskilful action. Surely it is not all just psychology masquerading as religion? Visualizing light pouring over us can't purify us of our actions, can it?

There is a power at work here that is mysterious and mercurial. There is something ineffable that can occur when one builds an authentic relationship with these qualities, particularly when one's motivation is altruistic in nature. This is strengthened greatly when one is introduced to them in a formal manner, for instance by a spiritual teacher during an ordination ceremony.

Delving into mantra with the heart and mind, dedicating oneself to the contemplation of a Bodhisattva image, reading inspiring verses that lead one to change can elevate us beyond the mire of past actions. By choosing these acts of devotion, we are making ourselves open and receptive to a positive influence.

Is it us doing the work? Is it an outside force? Again, false distinctions are not useful here. You are part of the universe. You can be kind. Therefore, we might say kindness is within. Kindness can also be demonstrated by others, so clearly kindness exists outside of us too. Maybe kindness just is. Kindness is a potentiality that exists in beings. Dedicating oneself to kindness, for example, is seeing that it is universal, not owned, not possessed. Kindness is one aspect of a protector and of our own potential.

Regardless of whether we believe in the existence of protectors, opening ourselves up to scrutiny and honestly appraising our behaviour is immensely liberating. Though painful, it can enable us to move beyond unfruitful habits and make more skilful choices in the future.

4. Dying to live

Giving up both a habit and the sometimes self-punishing thoughts about the habit can be very hard, particularly when they have been a part of our lives for so long. Habits can seem so entrenched that we identify with them. It is important that we commit to change; to do that, we need to renounce the habit, let it die, and know how to replace the habit with something more in line with our ideals.

There are many themes in the spiritual life that we revisit again and again. The thread that is relevant here is spiritual death. Spiritual death is not the ending of one's spiritual career, as in you move on from one faith to another. No, this is a practice of dying to one's past and being reborn into a new life.

We have already touched on this when considering the six realms of becoming. Between lives and within a life, we can be reborn in any one of the realms. Spiritual death reveals to us that change, even painful change, is essential to growth. A seed must die to produce the seedling. Leaves must fall to sustain the tree through the winter. Dying, letting go, passing on – however you frame it – is essential to living a full and meaningful life.

This process of spiritual death can take many forms, some simple, some elaborate. One way to begin this process of change is to mark it with a ritual. Remember that a ritual is rooted in common values and is shared by others of like mind.

Before attempting this ritual, select something about yourself that you actually do want to change, or let go of. More than that, contemplate your life without that particular stain upon it. How might you get to this point? Visualize that path, and start finding out how you might bring it into being before you begin this ritual. People tend to think that making resolutions at a certain time – like the New Year – will be enough for new habits to flourish. It is not. This ritual needs to be empowered by your own efforts to be free.

For example, if you find yourself overeating and want to live a healthier life, start putting changes in place before the ritual. Empty cupboards of tempting treats. Renew that gym membership. Contact that friend who also wants to try. Then you are ready for the ritual to start.

Alternatively, contemplate a quality that you already possess but wish to make more of. Commit, say, to practising mindfulness more in all aspects of life. You might decide to eat more mindfully and savour the experience of food. This is still a form of spiritual death, though it is not the habit that is 'dying' but the lack of engagement with the skilful habit.

In preparation for this ritual, begin with paying homage to the Three Jewels. Go for refuge by turning your mind to the true value of the Buddha, the Dharma, and the Sangha for you. Reciting the formal verses may help in this regard.

Then sit with your life as it is – your present state. Ask yourself one of these questions, whichever is most relevant to your situation:

- Is there some behaviour I do that needs to change to be in line with my aspirations?
- Am I remorseful about anything I have done to myself or others?
- Has someone been hurt by my actions?
- How might I make amends if they are needed?
- What am I putting in place to make more skilful choices?
- Is there something I do that could be cultivated further?

Go into the response to the question. Feel the discomfort or the release, or any other emotion that arises. Be strong. But be aware that you are not defined by these actions, or this response to them. This brings an aspect of wisdom to bear on the situation. You do not need to cling to the actions or the response. Generate metta (loving kindness) for yourself and those whom you may have hurt. Hold the experience with the two arms of wisdom and compassion. Nurture the seed of change.

Consider the action you wish to give up. Does it sit within the framework of the five precepts in their negative form? Is it a combination of them? That is possible too. Analyze the 'wrongdoing', the 'evil', in terms of the five precepts.

Take a piece of paper and find a way to record the unskilful act that you wish to give up. It could be a word, a phrase, or even an image, or just a mark that encompasses for you the act and its effects. As you draw or write, imagine the action bleeding onto the paper and leaving you. It need not be an essay. The intention is all.

Quietly recite the Avalokitesvara mantra to yourself or, if you are in a collective setting, join voices in chanting the mantra and evoking universal compassion. This ritual can be done when making offerings during a puja.

Take the piece of paper marked with your intention to let go of the habit, to let it die, and offer it before the shrine. You are bringing the 'evil' into the presence of the Three Jewels and the figures on the refuge tree. They, and those in the room with you, are witnessing your intention to renounce this action. The other participants may have no idea what it is, but you have a shared intention to relinquish whatever holds you back.

Burn the paper in a safe, fireproof receptacle. Allow it to be reduced to ash. When you return to your place, rest in the mantra and in your intention to move beyond the limits of the habit.

Will the cremation of a piece of paper, a piece of a past you would like to let go, purify you? No, burning paper is not going to magically cleanse you of past deeds, but the integrity of your approach to the practice and to its value will have an impact.

5. Something to try

Now we are able to practise the full Sevenfold Puja by ourselves. The first four sections or verses should be much clearer to you by this point. You can find a full version of the puja in the appendix at the end of the book, or you could purchase a copy that contains other practices, mantras, and rituals to assist your practice.

The remaining three verses – 'Rejoicing in merit', 'Entreaty and supplication', and 'Transference of merit' – may have more resonance now that the context has been explained in the previous chapters. In brief, as you take on reciting these additional verses, you are celebrating the best in others and asking for guidance on the path. Lastly, you are asserting an altruistic wish that whatever has been achieved is for the benefit of others, not solely for yourself.

In the next chapter, we will open to a whole new state, one freed from remorse. In the next chapter, we will encounter joy!

6. The chapter in review

- Evil in a Buddhist context is that which is in accordance with avarice, hatred, and ignorance.
- We must be courageous in seeing ourselves and the consequences of our actions.
- Karma is not fate or destiny.
- Confession is not about absolving ourselves from the consequences of our unskilful actions.
- Rituals of confession, whether elaborate or simple, are empowered by our deep remorse in conjunction with an awareness that we can change.

Chapter Ten

Rejoicing: What Am I Grateful For?

Anybody who has helped others is to be rejoiced in.
Instead of denigrating or debunking, as seems to be the
fashion, one appreciates and enjoys and feels happy in the
contemplation of other people's good qualities and deeds.

Sangharakshita, *The Bodhisattva Ideal*[61]

1. Negativity

In 2001, two researchers named a particular aspect of the human
psyche that they believed explains how we have survived as a species.
Paul Rozin and Edward Royzman coined the term 'negativity bias'
to explain the ways in which negative or painful experiences seem
to have a greater impact on people than positive ones.[62] Fear of
loss, rumination on failures (real or imagined), fixation on possible
worst-case scenarios and intensely risk-averse behaviours are all
informed, they posit, by the negativity bias. Some theorists propose
an evolutionary purpose behind this bias, claiming that, without it,
our earliest ancestors would have become extinct through repeated
recklessness.

Recent functional magnetic resonance imaging (or fMRI) has given
us tantalizing clues into which parts of our brain activate when we
look back on past failures and perceived threats to social standing. The
same parts are less activated when reflecting on success and positive

experiences. The duration of activity is also longer for more negative experiences. It is thought that a tendency to provide more attention to the painful and negative is a means of guiding the individual away from conditions that could bring about similar experiences. So there is an imperative to analyze mistakes in the hopes of avoiding similar outcomes. In evolutionary terms, the ancestor who remembered and revisited a near encounter with a predator was more likely to learn from the experience and survive or avoid such an encounter in the future. Nihilists and pessimists might feel vindicated by this theory.

Perhaps the negativity bias is a remnant of an earlier stage of human evolution? Our brains contain structures common to other animals that regulate aspects of our behaviour in similar ways. The amygdala is one such part that is associated with more primal emotional states such as fear and aggression, as well as aspects of memory. From an evolutionary standpoint, the amygdala, as part of the limbic system, played an essential role in survival by igniting the fight-or-flight response. But being human is surely more than being able to run from this century's equivalent of a sabre-toothed tiger?

The danger with this, as with any mental phenomena, is that rumination becomes obsessive or even addictive. Seeing one's lived experience only through this negative lens is little different from seeing the world through rose-coloured glasses. Neither is a true depiction of the human world. Both are delusions. Out of the six realms explored in Chapter 7, the human realm is said to be one that has a relative balance of positive and negative experiences. To live a fully human life is not to avoid pain and challenge, but neither is it to stay deeply mired in them. The negativity bias may be a self-protecting mechanism, but challenging that biological conditioning is possible. By seeing joy, seeing love, celebrating talents we can train the mind to take us beyond merely surviving – we can begin to truly live in a less monochromatic world. Rejoicing in our own merits trains us to see our own breadth – our skills, our talents, our failings, and our traumas. We begin to see the truth, a balanced truth of who we are.

A fully human life, according to the Buddha, is one that invites us to be aware and connected in the experience of both pleasure and pain, joy and loss. As we have seen in the sections exploring the bhavacakra (wheel of becoming) and Avalokitesvara, a human life is a blend of ups and downs – one cannot be truly human without the light and the shade. We can reach for the stars in the morning and wallow in the mud by the afternoon. We can cry tears of joy and of misery – this is our human heritage. This does not debunk or dismiss the negativity bias, but seeks to round it out a little.

Though I am not a neuroscientist or cognitive researcher, I still wonder about the ways in which we learn from past mistakes. This may have something to do with my profession as an educator. It is true that negative experiences can shock us into changing our ways, but some of the most powerful learning experiences I can recall are based on an embodied sense of joy and excitement. Singing in choirs, acting on stage, playing collaborative games, teaching Dharma classes – all have been powerfully integrating and threat-free experiences that have helped me feel alive. How do these fit in with Rozin and Royzman's theory? I felt the 'rightness' of this theory, but wanted to put it to the test.

2. One jewel at a time

At a workplace some years ago, I set up an experiment to explore these questions. It was very revealing, if a bit unpopular at first. I placed three jars on the communal table in the staffroom. One jar contained coloured glass jewels. It was unlabelled. The other two were empty but had very specific labels. One read 'Moaning and Complaining', and the other read 'Gratitude and Appreciation'. The idea was for people to move a glass jewel or bead from the unlabelled jar into the appropriately labelled one when they were either talking at the table or passing through. People were encouraged to pop a bead in if they were despairing of a student's progress or griping about a staff member's thoughtlessness. Similarly, if they saw acts of kindness or were helped by others and wanted to express that, there was a jar to receive that bead. In both cases, people could decide whether to share what was happening out loud or just internalize it as they placed the bead in the jar. You might imagine which jar was filled first. It confirmed the pervasiveness of negativity at least!

Further complaints came that the 'Moaning and Complaining' jar was punishing people for expressing themselves. (Punishing was not meant to be part of the experiment.) Surely venting is important? A good point, so I suggested that, before adding new beads from the blank jar to the 'Gratitude and Appreciation' jar, we remove them from the 'Moaning and Complaining' jar first. The miserable jar quickly emptied and stayed relatively low in the remaining months. The point had been made. It is easy to whinge, but harder to see the beauty in things that hold such potential for wonder. It also highlighted how hard it is to change an established culture of negativity. Eventually, we only had the 'Gratitude and Appreciation' jar, and a much more positive environment was established in the staffroom.

People began to challenge their habits of negativity. Sometimes, if teachers were having a particularly challenging day, they would seek me and the jar out and look for positives. In these instances, the person might be delving deep, struggling to see the silver lining in the cloud that was their day, but they would leave the interaction with a smile and a sense that someone had witnessed them. And there, in the jar, was evidence that the day was not all bad. No day ever is. Hope survives when there is an opportunity to cultivate it.

Now, at the Buddhist primary and high school where I work, we have daily 'Jewel in the Jar' moments. When students engage in positive pro-social behaviours inspired by kindness, appreciation, compassion, or equanimity, a jewel is added to a communal jar. This becomes an ongoing visual representation of positive acts – a tally of 'good karma', as it were. When the jar is filled, the students are rewarded with an activity of their choosing. Pizza parties are a popular choice!

Jewels are never removed from the jar as a punishment. That would undermine the value of teaching young people to value positive actions over criticism and negativity. To emphasize the positive is to say that good can triumph, that love can defeat hate, and that your actions build towards something wonderful. Children need to have that paradigm affirmed. So do many adults in this tired and cynical world.

It is easy to find faults. Whole disciplines of thought have developed around ways of critiquing and viewing phenomena, whether in the sciences or in the arts. Deficiencies are pointed out daily in education, politics, and business, far more than the successes are celebrated. This negativity is fine-tuned in the media, and weaponized into making us hungry consumers. If we are unhappy and tense at all the negativity we perceive, we will seek to alleviate that pain through the popularized means available – buying things. Buying things we enjoy gives us a sense of achievement, and releases the appropriate neurochemicals into our brains, which helps us to feel good. But what happens when the truth hits us, that no amount of purchasing will address the core questions of why we suffer? We may then feel let down and driven to find something else to buy to alleviate the pain. Temporarily of course. The cycle continues: we remain on the wheel of becoming, and keep circling through the six realms of pain, craving, surviving, and so on.

But what if we challenged the harping, critical paradigm by figuratively adding more beads to the jar of 'Gratitude and Appreciation'? If we were to celebrate the good, to rejoice in the fine qualities in ourselves and others on a regular basis, what would the world be like? Some would find such positivity nauseating at first, but, if the words were true and the intent was pure, surely such rejection of the concept would end soon enough. There may well be a negativity bias, but there is also a possibility for positivity.

I am not suggesting that we should live in denial of cruelty, deception, fraud, and negativity. These do exist, but how do we exist in relationship with them? Are we quick to sink in a mire of misery, or do we meet the reality of the situation and strive for a positive solution? Can we act skilfully in the face of what appear to be overwhelming odds? This is the life of a Bodhisattva – a being set on the path of Enlightenment for all beings. They see what is needed, but also what is already present.

3. Rejoicing in merit

'Jewel in the Jar' moments appear within the puja in the form of rejoicing in merit. This is the stage in the puja, after we have acknowledged our ethical faults, when we open to a wider picture –

the world is filled with people who do act ethically, who do inspire us, who practise the spiritual life wholeheartedly. Here we move beyond remorse and experience joy.

The verses from the Sevenfold Puja are as follows:

I rejoice with delight
In the good done by all beings,
Through which they obtain rest
With the end of suffering.
May those who have suffered be happy!

I rejoice in the release of beings
From the sufferings of the rounds of existence;
I rejoice in the nature of the Bodhisattva
And the Buddha,
Who are Protectors.

I rejoice in the arising of the Will to Enlightenment,
And the Teaching:
Those oceans that bring happiness to all beings,
And are the abode of welfare of all beings.

Some of the wording here echoes earlier sections. To 'obtain rest with the end of suffering' is synonymous with Enlightenment itself. This refers to the truth that others have attained Enlightenment, proving it is possible. Think back to our exploration of the three fetters or chains that hold us back, and you have a sense of what this verse is alluding to.

The phrase 'the release of beings from the sufferings of the rounds of existence' reminds us of the work of compassion in the six states of being. These states are dominated by pleasure, avarice, torture, ignorance, survival, and addiction. To be released from them is to embrace the Dharma path and free oneself from greed, hatred, and delusion. Compassion manifests in a myriad of ways depending on the situation: it is not a 'one size fits all' quality.

We encountered the bodhicitta, or will to Enlightenment, before in its depiction as a deep blue jewel held in the hands of Avalokitesvara. There are two kinds of bodhicitta – the conceptual and the active.

The conceptual is the mental attitude and intention to practise for the welfare of others. The other is the actual practices you engage in to bring that about. In the tradition, one form is known as the absolute bodhicitta and the other is the relative bodhicitta. Puja works on developing that aspirational, conceptual form known as the absolute. How we choose to enact that outside of the puja is the relative bodhicitta. So how do we take the aspiration into our relationships with others and the world? What do we do to be of true service?

'The abode of welfare' is a reference to going for refuge. This is a safe place, where beings can be nurtured. As we saw in Chapter 8, going for refuge on the outer level is a formal recitation; on the inner level, it is an understanding of the Buddha, Dharma, and Sangha's place in a Buddhist life. On a practical level, we apply the example of the Buddha's life, his teaching, and the values of the Buddhist community in the expectation that, through consistent and applied effort, we may embody the Three Jewels in all that we do.

4. Rejoicing

You could consider the previous stage, confession of faults, as the real purpose behind puja. After all, here is an opportunity to look at yourself openly and commit to change. But to see this ritual as about personal catharsis is to miss the point. Puja is not solely a practice of perfecting the self: it helps us spend less time asserting self-interest. But more on that when we come to the final verse of the puja.

Making the puja all about ourselves is a common failing, and it is easy to see why. You make the shrine, you bow, you perform the salutations, and you go for refuge. It is a personal commitment to follow the teaching and to practise the precepts. Even the words 'with deeds of loving kindness I purify my body' emphasize the personal aspect of practice. The honest contemplation of one's failings when confessing is personal. But this all occurs in a much larger context. Rejoicing in merit fleshes this out.

Rejoicing in merit provides even more context to the spiritual life, broadening the scope of the practice. Yes, there are protectors,

Bodhisattvas, wise teachers from the tradition from whom we can draw inspiration, but there are also others who are possessed of similar aspirations and have made progress along the path. These may be people close to us. These could be ordained Buddhists or fellow practitioners. There might be teachers from other traditions whose works you admire. This is an opportunity to reflect on these individuals and their positive qualities, and even to express gratitude that they have entered your life in some capacity.

I frequently reflect on a man who was born in Tibet back in the twelfth century. He was brought up in the mountains in harsh conditions, treated poorly by relatives, and would have been driven to the point of suicide had it not been for the Dharma. He learned to relinquish negative habits, and was taught to see the way things really are, just as the Buddha saw them. This simple Tibetan farmer could easily have remained unknown to me – I would have heard nothing of his inspiring life of fortitude and compassion were it not for those who heard his story, passed it on, wrote it down, translated and published it in a language I can understand. Thousands of people's devotion and effort are behind me hearing his name one time in a shrine room on a retreat in the early 2000s. And I was also ready to hear that name and have my heart opened. What a miracle that the life of a man hundreds of years ago, who lived in a remote corner of the world, can touch mine today!

This is an everyday miracle that reflects the Buddha's teachings on conditionality. You are also connected to this Tibetan saint (Milarepa, if you are curious) and to all those who have come before you. Every time you bow to a shrine or sit in meditation, this has been done before and will be done again. We have already noted that puja is a re-enactment of encounters with the Buddha, and so you are, by virtue of knowing his name and some of his teachings, in contact with a man who lived in northern India 2,600 years ago. You do not speak his language, and he may never even have known your language existed, but he did know what we all have in common. He knew that our common experience is one of discomfort and dis-ease driven by conditions, but that there is a way to move from this ancestry of pain and into a new inheritance – Enlightenment. He inspired others to be better, to grow skilful qualities, and to put those qualities at the service of others. Everyone who has contacted the Dharma, in whatever way, is worthy of celebration.

Good qualities, as we have already explored, exist as potentials in human beings. Avalokitesvara's compassion is, in a sense, our own altruistic endeavour writ large. Whether we choose to see that potential and make something of it is up to us. Thankfully, we have meditation practices such as the metta bhavana – the cultivation of loving kindness – in which we can connect on an imaginal level with the good in others.

But, as Sangharakshita implies in the quote that opens this chapter, rejoicing in the good of others is in short supply. There are communities in the world whose primary currency is criticism. Why build something or someone up when tearing them/it apart is far more dramatic? A scalding meltdown on social media is bound to reach a larger audience than an encouraging tweet. Rejoicing in merits is an opportunity to redress this dangerous imbalance. Look for the good in others, and you will eventually find it, even if you find it easier to see the faults.

Rejoicing in merits encourages us to see the good in others. What do we rejoice in exactly? As stated above, we can rejoice in the fact that people have made contact with the Dharma, but we can also be more specific. We can consider the effort individuals have made to practise the precepts, to engage in meditation, and to tread the path of the Dharma. We can also rejoice in those who are not Buddhist but exhibit compassion and awareness. All who work for the good of others are worth celebrating. This extends to the Buddhas and the Bodhisattvas themselves, who are brought more acutely into our awareness by the skilful actions of others.

That person who gave you spare change to help you buy a coffee, the other who smiled and opened the door, the one who listened to you without proffering unsolicited advice, the singer who wrote a lyric that pierced your heart with kindness – all are worthy of being rejoiced in as much as the person teaching the Dharma class or the one who set up the chairs.

We can also rejoice in those who, regardless of the state they are in, are making efforts to change. Regardless of where people find themselves on the wheel of becoming – in a state of anguish or pleasure, or any of the other states – they make effort to endure, to thrive, to survive. Sure, some of their choices may be clouded by ignorance or confusion or self-interest, but they try to be better nonetheless. Their strategies may be flawed, but they at least have strategies.

When we consider the wheel of becoming that we explored earlier, it may be that we look upon the inhabitants of the various realms in a one-sided way – we focus on their pain and feel called to alleviate it. As noble as this is, it is only half the picture: to see others in their fullness, we need to see them for all the good they do as much as for the discomfort they experience. Avalokitesvara, as the Bodhisattva of compassion holding a crystal mala, encourages us to face up to each moment as it comes, whether pleasant or unpleasant. In one of Avalokitesvara's other hands there is a blooming flower, reminding us that growth and beauty are possible in even the simplest of moments. Both the mala and the flower are held high for us to notice: Avalokitesvara represents the ability to be present with and connected to anyone in any state. Beings going around and around the realms of existence are doing the best they can with what they know. This is worth noting, celebrating. There is something to rejoice in when beings exhibit fortitude, persistence, loyalty, and humility in the face of adversity.

Avalokitesvara's other pair of hands holds the bodhicitta to their heart. This is also worth cherishing and celebrating. We also rejoice in the bodhicitta – the will to Enlightenment that we explored earlier. As a quality, wanting and working for the Enlightenment of others is worthy of praise. Selfless activity is the highest value that one can rejoice in and celebrate.

So rejoicing is an opportunity to work against tendencies to see only the worst in others and ourselves. Rejoicing helps round out the picture so that we don't fall into feeling pity. Theoretically, we might see the value of rejoicing, but how can we give voice to our heartfelt response?

Within the Triratna Buddhist tradition, there are many opportunities for rejoicing. This is something that is encouraged in both small and large gatherings. Rejoicing happens when individuals stand up or are selected to take on positions of responsibility within Buddhist centres. Similarly, when people leave such positions, it is customary to celebrate their good qualities and achievements. This is done not to bolster egos but to acknowledge their commitment, creativity, and generosity.

This happens in smaller groups too, though not nearly enough. Congratulating others on points well articulated, thanking others for helping point out the errors in one's thinking, noting gentle acts of witnessing through difficult times could all become more regular practices. The danger is, of course, that such acts become habitual or, worse, become distorted into currying favour or gaining attention. This is where wise attention is needed to check one's motivation for rejoicing.

Even harder perhaps than offering rejoicing is to receive it gracefully. Some can tend to downplay compliments of this nature, or counter them with a rebuttal of some kind. Such humility is an unhelpful habit, as it denies the giver of the rejoicing an opportunity to practise generosity. The giving and receiving of praise are just as much about the deliverer as they are about the receiver.

I am a habitual blocker of praise, yet I seek it out far too much. It is a strange internal landscape to inhabit. Wanting approval but resisting or even distrusting the bestower of praise is deeply unsatisfying. It is with considerable effort that I train myself to accept what is offered with a simple 'thank you', though I confess that the inner response may be far from willing to be grateful. Each time I remember to simply accept compliments when they are offered, particularly if they are authentically earned, the fetter of habit is loosened. In this case, the habit is of needing but not feeling worthy of approval.

Consider this within your own life: what arises when someone rejoices in you and your qualities? Is the response born of kindness, generosity, and awareness of others? If so, a skilful act has occurred. If one is quick to dismiss, explain away, or even rebuke the speaker, the opposite values are in play and one is not being respectful to the speaker.

Both offering rejoicings and receiving them can be difficult, but the Buddha never suggested that walking the Dharma path was easy.

5. Something to try

Continue with a formal practice of the Sevenfold Puja as
often as you are able. The puja can be performed at any time
of the day or night. I sometimes perform it on the train on
the way to work as a means of clarifying my intention and
gaining perspective. Of course, I am not reciting it aloud
and lighting candles or making full-body prostrations on a
busy commuter train, but I am sitting quietly and imagining
the offerings whilst staying true to the meaning.

To practise rejoicing in merit, you could bring attention
to the positive qualities of others and consider ways in
which you could become a voice for rejoicing. You could
start small, perhaps noting down the fine qualities of others
and reflecting on them. Work up to small acts of verbal
recognition, and note the effect they have on the recipient
and yourself. Giving gifts and other tokens of appreciation
can also go a long way towards generating a new culture
of thankfulness and joy around you. I know from personal
experience how the simple act of offering a small gift can
shift your perspective of another person. You could even try
the glass bead experiment in your own workplace, but be
warned: not everyone is walking the same path as you.

6. The chapter in review

- Negative events in our lives have a potential to reorient
  us towards safety. This is not, however, the total of our
  experience.
- Certain communities and world views emphasize
  negativity, fear, and isolation.
- We can actively bring our attention to the positive, to more
  joyful experiences, and reap the rewards of connection and
  fulfilment.

- Rejoicing in the skills and talents of others, seeing the good done by those around us, however small, can help shape a more realistic view.
- Rejoicing is about actively witnessing the efforts, skills, and abilities of others.
- Compassion is cultivated when we notice the efforts people make and then give voice to our observations.
- Compassion need not be reserved for people in crisis.
- There are many ways to celebrate others and rejoice in their merits.
- Celebrating others can be challenging, but just as challenging is receiving praise and appreciation.

Chapter Eleven

Entreaty: How Do I Get the Help I Need?

A single word of truth
which calms the mind
is better to hear than a thousand
irrelevant words.

Dhammapada[63]

1. Entreaty and supplication: asking for help

Can you recall that pivotal moment when you set out on the spiritual path? A great sadness in my life is that I do not recall mine enough. Remembering why we started on the spiritual path can be a profound source of inspiration.

What was mine? It occurred at that same Buddhist temple where the nun hit me with a stick, but a year or so before that event. I was still a ritual magician at this time, and not yet disenchanted with it, or so I thought. This was on a day trip away from the city with friends to visit the largest Buddhist temple in the Southern Hemisphere, which happened to be an hour and a half south of Sydney.

The site was something to behold! It was as if the hands of a giant had scooped up a mountain temple in Taiwan and placed it gently on the slopes of an unassuming industrial estate. My brain could not quite comprehend the majestic orange tiled roofs rising above panel beaters' workshops and wooden pallet distributors. To the left of a roundabout, automotive repair and office supplies manufacturers;

to the right, a vibrantly coloured mountain gate and a winding path through weeping willows.

After fragrant refreshments in the teahouse, we climbed the central stairs to the sounds of the highway. There, at the top, through the incense smoke, I saw what changed my life forever.

Sometimes you don't know what you are missing until you encounter it – or, as in this case, it encounters you. Inside the smaller shrine room (not the one with the many Buddhas) was a standing figure in pastels and gold. It towered over us, looking at us with the gentlest of eyes, which were to all appearances glistening with tears. It was the eyes of the figure that I saw first, which is surprising given its more unusual features. There were arms, hundreds and hundreds of them – some were fully realized, and others were fanned out behind in a great stylized arc. Each arm ended in a delicately moulded hand, and in the palm of each hand was an eye.

I could not fully comprehend what I was seeing, but I stood transfixed, tears welling in my own eyes. I saw, no I felt, an inordinate amount of heaviness in my heart. This was not a cardiac event, but a sudden painful recollection of the harm I had caused myself and my partner over the years. The façade, the veil had been ripped off, perhaps by one of those hands. The figure saw me more fully than I was prepared to see myself. Time slowed, and I could not take my eyes from the image before me, despite the intense discomfort. And then my gaze shifted, and I saw that in many of the hands were implements – vases, flowers, swords, and other mysterious items. I knew, without a doubt, that this thousand-armed being had the thing I needed to feel whole and to make amends.

Even as I write this now, my eyes are wet and I am deeply grateful. This was my introduction to Avalokitesvara manifesting in the thousand-armed form. I saw them and they saw me. I saw myself with their compassionate eyes.

Did I discover which object would alleviate my pain? Yes, yes I did. I hope you find yours too.

But sometimes, frustratingly, our search for a solution is fruitless, or not timely enough for our liking. Why doesn't catharsis happen to our schedule? At other times, the medicine is bitter-tasting, or the advice offered is true, but a bit of a letdown – what do you mean I would be happier if I stopped hating myself?! I want a magic mantra or a tantric visualization practice to fix me, not that! We can search for the pith instructions that we believe will set us on the correct course, only to find that the teaching is unremarkable and, well, dull.

You might not be stuck, troubled, or burdened by life, but you can still ask for encouragement or support. You do not have all the answers, and neither do I. However, in reciting this next stage of the puja, the entreaty and supplication verses, we are recognizing that we are not alone, and we are humble enough to bow to those wiser than us.

In entreaty and supplication, we are asking for help and expressing gratitude. We are asking that the Dharma remain present, and not be supplanted by other things or by different views in our minds. This stage is both an affirmation of commitment and a request for continuity of influence. May I not drop the Dharma for some other activity. May the guidance offered by the Dharma remain present in our own lives, and not fade away or lose its power to inspire. So, too, may all who walk the path not be deterred from seeing it through to the end. We wish that the freedom we have to explore our path be made available to others, and that it long continue to be a source of guidance.

Who do we go to for guidance? Not everyone will have the experience I had with a statue. Each person's moment of asking for help is unique, though there are common threads to do with dissatisfaction, curiosity, a need to serve, or intense suffering, to name but a few. The Buddhist tradition contains a rich source of inspiration and support.

On one level, this part of the puja is about bringing to mind Buddhas and Bodhisattvas, and asking them to remain as sources of inspiration. Pragmatically, it's a wish to remember their names and appearance, or a hope to find images of them as you travel near and far, or to see new books written about them, or have talks delivered to give you new insights into how you might best come to experience them. This is a fervent wish that these symbols of the best in us, others, and the world continue to be potentials in the human consciousness.

But what kind of guidance is this?

You can receive instruction in meditation or on how to be more ethical to guide yourself on the Bodhisattva path. Guidance can also take the form of an honest friend who reflects back what they see and hear you doing with your life. Guidance informed by the protectors need not be a voice from the clouds or from the depths of meditative absorption: a silent witnessing or a firm intervention from a loving friend can be a small-'b' bodhisattva act.

Here are the entreaty and supplication verses to reflect on:

Saluting them with folded hands
I entreat the Buddhas in all the quarters:
May they make shine the lamp of the Dharma
For those wandering in the suffering of delusion!

With hands folded in reverence
I implore the conquerors desiring to enter Nirvana:
May they remain here for endless ages,
So that life in this world does not grow dark.

2. The heart of the matter

A key source of guidance in a puja is often a reading of spiritual import. Usually, at this juncture in the puja, after this verse, a reading from the vast canon of Buddhist texts will be offered to serve as a teaching upon which to reflect. It may be a sutta from the time of the Buddha or a selection from a dramatic Mahayana sutra. Songs of inspiration from Tibet or sage advice from more recent Buddhists are common.

It can be useful to consider these readings as direct messages from the original author or from the Bodhisattva or Buddha figure. They are, at this moment, speaking to you at your most focused, most generous, and most receptive. The person tasked with reading is the conduit for the guidance and, with this imaginative attitude, you can have a sense of the original speaker or writer's presence in the room.

Listening to these readings can often be a profound experience. The concentration one has developed up until this point is now brought to bear on this teaching. Personally, this is where I find myself the most concentrated and most present in a puja. When this is followed by the *Heart Sutra*, the possibility for real spiritual change is made clear.

There is very little one can say about the *Heart Sutra* other than to provide some basic context. For a long time, it has been regarded as the pinnacle of sacred texts of East Asian Buddhism, particularly in China and Japan. There is ongoing academic and scholarly debate about the origins of the text. Some researchers believe it to be a text of Indian descent, but others argue that it is a much later text composed solely in China. Debate continues to this day as to its time and place of origin.

The sutra recounts a meditative experience or practice engaged in by the Bodhisattva Avalokitesvara. In an absorbed state, Avalokitesvara observes that phenomena appear real but are inherently lacking in coherent and substantial essence. This applies to all phenomena, including mental events and internal experiences. They have the illusion of independent existence, but are void of a solid unchanging form. Words and names, while having a relative value, do not hold the essence of the conditioned phenomena being described. (This harks back to the lessons we learned from Scott McCloud and Magritte in Chapter 4.) This is a source of profound insight for Avalokitesvara, and, potentially, for us. This discovery is then referred to as the 'great perfection' or even 'perfecting practice', which enables all who seek Buddhahood to reach it.

For a considerable time, this sutra was regarded as a debate between the view of the Hinayana and that of the Mahayana, with the Mahayana triumphing over the non-existent voice of its opponent. Avalokitesvara, in this reading, is the victor, with the philosophical perspective of the Mahayana doctrine of emptiness proving no match for the other. Later Buddhism is seen as triumphing over earlier Buddhist philosophy. One scholar suggests, however, that this sutra may not be laying forth a foundational thesis on the nature of reality and espousing a particular doctrine, but recounting a specific meditation practice and its fruits. This view sees the sutra as a meditative journal entry, an account of a meditation experience rather than an expository discourse on the non-nature of phenomena.[64]

Regardless of whether it is a doctrinal statement or an account of a method, the *Heart Sutra* is a potent enquiry into our very nature.

When we investigate our experience, we do find 'something', yet that something too is composed of 'somethings' that are not of the same form as the original object of investigation. These 'somethings' also dissolve upon analysis. We are left with powerful existential questions – who are we? What are we? We clearly exist, but is what we see the truth? The three fetters are seriously weakened when contemplation of the *Heart Sutra* is a part of your spiritual life.

There are many books and commentaries on the *Heart Sutra*, including a section on it in Sangharakshita's guide to Buddhist canonical literature called *The Eternal Legacy*.[65] From it, one can see just how many treasures of the Dharma are waiting for us to turn to for advice.

3. Seeing

We can seek guidance by reading the Dharma or attending classes, or by delving deep into meditation. Another way is to do what millions have done for millennia – give attention to devotional images and forms. Before the age of mass media or even the printed word, images spoke to the hearts and minds of devotees around the world.

The earliest images of the Buddha in human form are from the first century CE. A particularly fine example is a golden reliquary now housed in the British Museum, which depicts the Buddha flanked by two Hindu deities who are making obeisance to him. (An assertion of Buddhism's superiority in the mind of the creator, perhaps?) This is the earliest depiction of the historical Buddha that can be dated. Prior to that, the Buddha was depicted through symbols, including images of the bodhi tree, an empty throne, or a stylized version of his footprints.

Some of the evocative early Buddhas come to us from what is now northern Pakistan, which in the first century was a significant place along the Silk Road trade routes. Here, Buddhism encountered a melting pot of art, culture, and style. The Buddhas created in this region reflect the influences coming to the East along that road: they resemble Greek or Roman statues, as we saw earlier. These Buddhas are handsome, exquisitely carved god-like figures with robes sculpted to resemble togas. Though retaining elements of Indian features, these Buddhas are more like representations of the Greek Adonis.

Approaching Enlightenment

Buddhism travelled widely across Asia in the early centuries CE, and, whatever culture it met, the prevailing art forms, technologies, and tastes shaped how people imagined the Buddha. This accounts for the Buddha appearing Chinese in China, Japanese in Japan, and so forth. People wanted the Buddha to be like them, perhaps to make him more relatable as a person and as a teacher. After all, the Buddha was clear that we each have the potential for Enlightenment, to be Buddhas, so why not help that process along in an imaginative sense by showing the result? In the West, however, the depiction of the Buddha has not followed this established pattern.

It is interesting that in the West, with the painful history of colonialism and cultural appropriation, the fashion is for Buddhas to remain 'foreign' in appearance. Buddhas frequently appear as decor in fashionable dwellings, suggesting something mystical, or as souvenirs from excursions to exotic locations. These objects are often imitations of existing archeological relics, affirming their 'otherness' or 'orientalism'. Buddha and Bodhisattva images can easily be hoarded as esoteric bric-a-brac or as part of an art collection. For the Western postcolonial intellectual, Buddhas are much easier to accept as art than as images of devotion. Speaking broadly, if we keep Buddhas and Buddhism 'foreign', we keep the Dharma at arm's length. We maintain a safe distance from its potential, but we can still derive a pleasant aesthetic experience from the images. This is Buddhism as a thing you own, not a thing you do.

As stated earlier, it is easier to own a Buddha than to become one. If we believed Buddhahood was a feasible proposition and much more than a lifestyle accessory, we'd take the Buddha off the mantle and place him in our holy of holies – whatever that is for us. We'd even consider depicting Buddhas more like us if we thought ourselves capable of becoming one. Of course, I am not suggesting a process of 'white-washing' the historical Buddha – he was clearly a northern Indian man – and so depictions of Shakyamuni Buddha as a person I believe should reflect the appropriate ethnicity. However, the representation of Buddha nature in an image could be more diverse. Experimentation with depicting more Eurocentric

Buddhas has been met with varying results, yet even these point towards what the Buddha image is trying to teach us.

Regardless of the ethnic appearance of Buddha images, it is important to sit with these figures and allow them to speak. Each image of a Buddha or Bodhisattva is a complex code of teachings, associations, and layers of meaning. Some embody whole traditions of meditation or action, or even of thought. These levels of meaning only become clear over years of reflection and devotion. New associations form regularly, which is why these images have existed for so long as dynamic sources of inspiration.

But the images are not signs that have easily communicated meanings. It would be far too easy to dissect them into their constituent parts and stick with that, as if in naming something one has mastered the 'knowing' it contains. This is a valuable exercise, to understand the parts, but not at first. Like meeting someone for the first time, we need to take them in and connect. See if we have anything in common. Resting in the presence of a Buddha or Bodhisattva outside of an analytical, expository mind is an important aspect of devotion.

It is valuable to sit with an image of a Buddha or Bodhisattva and allow them to speak to us. I'm not suggesting that the form will talk, though stranger things have happened: no, the suggestion is to ask questions of the object and allow you to build your own personal relationship.

One way to do this is to apply an adaptation of some thinking routines developed by Harvard University's Project Zero,[66] which are designed to move us into a deep relationship with an image or symbol.

4. Something to try

#1

The first one to try is called 'Looking: ten times two', and is used to make detailed observations that push past first impressions, judgements, and opinions.

To do this, you need some time, a pencil, and some paper, and, of course, an image of a Buddha or Bodhisattva figure.

1. Look at the image quietly for at least thirty seconds. Let your eyes wander over the image. Note the grasping mind that is making 'I like' and 'I don't like' comments about the image. Place those judgements to one side, and return to observing the image.
2. List ten words or phrases about any aspect of the image. These could also be questions. Allow your mind to be associative as well – let details, colours, and shapes suggest other objects, colours, shapes, or even moods.
3. Repeat steps 1 and 2: look at the image again, and try to add ten more words or phrases to your list.

#2

After you have tried this and pushed yourself to see the image more carefully, perhaps even seeing things that were not readily apparent, it can be useful to get a second opinion or even a third. The 'Elaboration game' thinking routine (also from the Harvard Graduate School of Education) asks you to meet with two others. Usually this is done based around one image, but it can be useful to see connections and correlations across images too.

1. You identify a specific section of the image, and describe what you see. Be detailed in describing, in words, what you observe. You also add what it makes you think about or contemplate.
2. Another person then elaborates on your observations by adding more detail about the section and asking clarifying questions. They may see what you see, or something entirely different.

3. A third person elaborates further by adding yet
    more detail, and suggesting further questions and
    observations.

This is a way to see more clearly what an image may be both concealing from the inattentive and revealing to those who take the time to look deeply.

Perhaps the most important aspect of being present with an image of this kind is to move beyond those 'I like' and 'I don't like' statements. These create cognitive boundaries that close you off from accepting the teaching being offered in the image. Moving beyond such boundaries is another way we can shake free of the fetters of habit, superficiality, and vagueness. Habit is defeated by not going with the first opinion, superficiality is reduced by giving close attention, and vagueness is disempowered by discussing and clarifying your understanding.

Another way to look at an image and be suffused with what it is trying to communicate is to draw, paint, or colour it. For centuries, temples and monasteries have run schools to train artists to adorn the spaces with images of Enlightenment. These schools – teaching statue making or the painting of scrolls called thangkas – have kept the iconography much the same, allowing each symbolic aspect a chance to be passed to a new generation. And, of course, sold to new generations of visitors seeking a spiritual icon to which to devote their lives.

Though of course, you could make your own! There are many commercially available colouring books that are used to promote mindfulness. Some contain images of mandalas and even Buddhas or Bodhisattvas. They are of variable quality and accuracy, so be discerning if you choose to take up a practice of colouring as a means of gaining insight into a particular figure.

Just a sidenote on this: colouring in is not a childish practice. Colouring in is a means of holding your attention mindfully on an object of awareness. To make an image of this kind and keep your attention on it as you do so helps imprint it on your consciousness. This is a practice that I engaged in as part of my ordination training. It was immensely useful in helping me recall the figures on the Triratna refuge tree.

5. Reading

There is a lot one can read about the Buddhas and Bodhisattvas too. This can be very useful to gain a sense of their place in the canonical literature and in Buddhist history. Moreover, it can be valuable to help decipher and access the more hidden aspects of the iconography. But reading comes with an important caveat. Words, definitions, and descriptions are not the Buddha, Bodhisattva, or other protector. This echoes the insights Avalokitesvara came to in the *Heart Sutra* and the more mundane artistic comments made by Magritte and McCloud. Words are a tether to help us understand something that cannot easily be contained.

Words are also inaccurate and deceptive. The words 'blue sky' are descriptive, but are not the reality of 'blue' or 'sky', let alone the 'blue sky' itself. 'Blue' is not blue even if written in blue ink, for the word itself approximates or rather points to what we perceive as blueness. The blueness is separate from the writing of the word in blue. Subtle variations of the structure of our own eyes mean that no one is truly able to see the same blue as anyone else. As for 'sky', the sky is not even a thing – it is an insubstantial phenomenon. The sky is not only a conglomeration of gases, but also a matter of perspective.

The sky is above, but, when one is in the sky or above the atmosphere, there is no sky at all. Sky cannot be touched or tasted or heard, yet we perceive it with the eye. Sometimes it is apparent and other times not, but we believe it to be there behind the storm clouds.

Moreover, the sky we see is not actually blue – that is a by-product of an interaction between wavelengths of light and charged particles in the atmosphere. A blue sky is not a thing to be named, but a process in constant spontaneous co-arising. The actual experience of a blue sky only exists when all of these factors, including the attention of the perceiver, are present. The words 'blue sky' only point to the true magic occurring.

So too, compassion is an abstract noun that is different from innumerable expressions of compassion in the world. The word is not the act. At what point does a mother's compassion for their child begin? In the womb, or before that when contemplating the love they might one day show to a child? Is compassion in the eyes of lovers meeting as they create life? Where does this flicker of a hope of having a child to love even originate? And is there compassion in scolding the child? Where might that love go when the child, now an adolescent, disobeys the rules? Compassion is not the word – it is a myriad actions intersecting in a complex web.

Words are not the thing to which they refer, yet they hold immense power. This is perhaps why mantras have such an impact: they express a meaning that is not accessed in the same way as other more functional words are.

Bearing all that in mind, it is true that words and reading can assist with clarifying and informing the reader about elements of the iconography that are embedded in unfamiliar cultural frameworks. This is particularly true of the Indo-Tibetan images, which have lineages of symbolic meaning that cannot easily be accessed by an untrained or uninformed mind.

6. Something else to try

Select an image of a Buddha or Bodhisattva that appeals to you, or perhaps one that is confusing. Or you might select a few, turn them over, and then choose one at random to be the object of your interest for the week.

Follow the thinking routines described above, and spend time reflecting on the image and the associations you have with it. Do not rush to tether the figure to the words of others in the early stages. Listen to the mantra of the figure, if indeed it has one. Then, do some reading with the intention of building even more curiosity. Find out about some of the gestures or colours, and explore those in detail, never forgetting that your initial responses are valid and not to be dispensed with.

If you can, find an image of the figure to colour in, taking time each day to add a little more detail. It does not have to be perfect or finished in any particular time frame.

You could introduce this Buddha or Bodhisattva to your shrine. Enjoy getting to know them and yourself a little more. Eventually, contemplating a Buddha image might even become like looking into a mirror.

It is worth approaching any exploration of this kind with a generous, enquiring mind. Share your interests with fellow Buddhists, and perhaps engage in dialogue about the Buddha figures that you feel drawn to. This can help you to clarify misunderstandings, and it may also inspire others and spark their curiosity.

7. The chapter in review

- You are not alone in the Dharma life.
- The *Heart Sutra* is a short but powerful text containing a number of concise teachings that ask us to question the conventions of what we perceive as reality.
- Through spending time with images of Buddhas and Bodhisattvas, we can come to understand and eventually embody the practices they represent.
- Studying and reading about Buddha images can assist in understanding what the iconography is pointing to.

Chapter Twelve

Dedication: How Far Will Ritual Take Me?

What nobility of feeling! To sacrifice your own pleasure to preserve the comfort of others! It is a thing, I confess, that would never occur to me.

Susanna Clarke, *Jonathan Strange & Mr Norrell*[67]

1. Dedication

May the merit gained
In my acting thus
Go to the alleviation of the suffering of all beings.
My personality throughout my existences,
My possessions,
And my merit in all three ways,
I give up without regard to myself
For the benefit of all beings.

Just as the earth and other elements
Are serviceable in many ways
To the infinite number of beings
Inhabiting limitless space;
So may I become
That which maintains all beings
Situated throughout space,
So long as all have not attained
To peace.

The final lines of this ritual, after everything we have offered and faced, unlikely as it seems, tell us that there is still more to give. We give everything up. Everything. Even our very bones, breath, and blood. Not literally, but symbolically.

Like Avalokitesvara in the *Heart Sutra*, we come to the point in our practice where we hold on to nothing whatever, or at least contemplate what that might be like. In some ways, this is the end of us – but the smaller us, not the greater one that was there all along, though there have been many passings and renunciations all through the puja.

We have died to miserliness by making offerings to someone who really has no perceivable need of them. We have acknowledged our place in a lineage of practitioners going backwards and forwards in time. In so doing, we have expanded the boundaries of ourselves. Confessing is clearly about dying to past habits and understanding that there is more to us than our unskilful actions, because we rejoice in our goodness. And the teaching of the *Heart Sutra*, which is unequivocal in its radical vision, has shown us we are not what we think we are, and neither are our thoughts what we think they are. We are thus free to shed who we were and just give ourselves and all we have to others. Consider this verse as a series of questions rather than statements, and you have a sense of how to begin realizing this stage of the puja:

- Do I act in accord with the aspiration to free others from suffering?
- To what degree am I selfless and generous in all I do?
- How far am I prepared to go to help others?
- Do I act as a protector to people?

As we have seen before, it is easy to be highly critical and judgemental when answering these questions. Short of Buddhahood itself, you will fall short. Similar to the verse on confession, here is an opportunity to give an honest appraisal of your practice. Yes, you might be unwilling to risk your own life for a stranger, but you might, after some years of meditation and Dharma study, be less reactive when they ask for help. That is a step along the journey towards the summit of Enlightenment.

In answering these questions honestly, we have the possibility of change if we act as the magician and transform the problem into the solution. Example? My response to the first question – 'Do I act in accord with the aspiration to free others from suffering?' – is, 'No, not always'. But, to transform this answer, I could consider what actions I actually do that are in line with the aim. *I enjoy listening and being open to others when they are communicating their distress.* There's the way I could be even more generous, even more of service – listen more. Rather than mire myself in believing I don't live up to my aspirations, I can turn that absence into presence and a path.

2. The elements

We may not notice a passing reference to the 'elements' in this verse, but this would be a missed opportunity. To seize this, we need to come full circle, just like the ouroboros belt worn by the Magician: we return to the subject of Chapter 1 – magic.

Anyone familiar with the basics of magic will be aware of the elements. In magical communities, these are understood to be the four foundational building blocks of the magical and phenomenal world. What is not generally known is that the significance of the four elements – earth, water, fire, and air – at least in the Western magical traditions, is a relatively late development. They come to us in philosophical writings from the fifth century BCE. It is in the fragmented writings of the philosopher and poet Empedocles (born around 495 BCE) that the theory of the four elements first appears. Building on the earlier works of Thales of Miletus and Heraclitus, Empedocles argued that a combination of earth, water, fire, and air constituted the nature of all things.

According to Empedocles, the four elements were not fixed but in constant change and flux, in a process of combining and reforming. They existed for a time, and then blended or merged with other elements to form new compounds. The elements were a collection of properties rather than discrete objects, and moods, emotions, thoughts, and attitudes also possessed these changeable attributes. The fire element manifested in anger, the water element in grief, earth in inflexibility, and wind in the sighs of love. However, all were fleeting and changing. Empedocles makes this clear in his poem 'On nature':

The Elements never cease their continuous running-
through, at one time coming together in love into a unity
and, at another, breaking up in hate [...] in this way, they
do not have a substantive nature and a lasting time of life,
but in so far as they never cease their continuous running-
through, in that way, they possess a time of life that is
unmoved in their cycles.[68]

However, the model of the elements is far older and more
sophisticated than the Ancient Greek Sicilian envisaged. The Buddha
himself adapted the early Vedic teaching of the elements long before
Empedocles, taking it far further than the simple model of changing
propensities, and expanding the four elements to six:

These are the six properties: the earth property, the liquid
[water] property, the fire property, the wind [air] property,
the space property, the consciousness property.[69]

That's right: six, not four. Two other properties must be present for
the first four to arise – there must be space for them to arise in or
occupy, and a capacity for them to be comprehended, co-created,
or observed. Therefore, earth arises only when there is a place for it
to manifest and a mind to perceive/apprehend it. The addition of
consciousness as an element is incredibly profound – the outer and
the inner worlds are mutually interdependent.

In the *Dhatu-vibhanga Sutta*, the Buddha remarks that one way to
gain and maintain discernment, the ability to really see with clarity,
is to observe how the elements arise and pass away within our direct
experience. Nothing remains fixed and constant. We do not own any of
these qualities, since they are, as Empedocles said later, in a state of flux.
We *experience* the properties of the elements, but we do not *possess* them.

Like Empedocles, the Buddha did not conceive of the elements
as solely external properties of the phenomenal world. In the *Maha-
Rahulovada Sutta*, the Buddha instructs his own son Rahula about the
six elements, and encourages him to investigate them both within his
direct experience and as a means of disengaging from distractions.
Here Rahula is encouraged to investigate the elements as a means of
cultivating much more refined states of consciousness.[70] The Buddha

Approaching Enlightenment

is encouraging Rahula, and us, to look deeply, to investigate, to observe the flow of wanting and disliking, and to be present without expecting things to be anything other than what they are.

To experience the elements and to relinquish them, we need to first have a lived sense of their qualities. They manifest in a variety of painful, pleasurable, and neutral ways in your experience. The table below, inspired by Sangharakshita's writing on the elements,[71] explores how these six manifest as external and internal propensities or elements. Which do you have greater or lesser awareness of or even mastery over?

Element	Manifesting as	Aspect
Earth	Solidity, inflexibility, connected, stable, grounded, resistant, form	Cohesion
Water	Movement, fluid, ebb and flow, ease, comfort, change, feeling	Undulation
Fire	Enthusiasm, inspiration, agitation, transformation, emotion	Radiation
Air	Flexibility, expansion, retraction, curiosity, floating, speech	Vibration
Space	Openness, broad, unconfined, freedom, potential, unfixedness	Location
Consciousness	Perceiving, discerning, appreciating, kind/ critical, limitless	Creation

Regarding the elements, it is a sobering reminder that, upon our death, the constituent elements of the body return to the world to be of use in some form. Our flesh and bones either decompose into the soil or are cremated to be stored or scattered and returned to the biosphere. Our ashes become the soil from which weeds or flowers grow. The fluids in our body are drained away and evaporate to join the atmosphere. The water that once pumped in our veins will rain upon hydrangeas in Cornwall and be boiled for tea in Venezuela. The air expelled from our lungs will brush the cheeks of monarchs and newborn children. Even the spaces we have occupied – the chair at our favourite coffee shop, our homes, our beds – are vacated to be inhabited by others.

Some may find this a sobering or confronting realization: nothing we have or hold on to is ours forever – the Sephora diamond necklace, the limited-edition Air Jordans, even this very body we inhabit are on loan; so why cling? We can live with an awareness that everything we are and own is borrowed, and at one time in the past and in the future it has belonged/will belong to others.

I have a tangible sense of this. My mother died last year, and I am in the process of sorting through her effects and my own grief. Given her tendency to hoard the most purposeless things, this sorting never seems to end. The letter opener that caught her eye on a trip to Norfolk Island in 1961 is buried in a drawer beneath decades of correspondence. Alabaster lamps whose wiring failed in 1983 are in boxes within boxes, within suitcases filled with tinsel and rubber bands. Each artefact is more than a souvenir. Each is a moment of seeing, wanting, holding, treasuring.

And, after a while, the things are a source of disappointment, loss, abandonment, and forgetting. The objects themselves are an echo of her, a piece of her. These objects were, in part, constituents of the story of her almost as much as her physical being was. As I sort through the pieces into the various piles – for the charity shop, for sale, for relatives, for me – these moments of connection with them are dispersed. The Princess Diana memorial mug, the Wedgwood plate, the unopened wedding presents will become part of the story of others or decompose in landfill. In dispersing these things, I am discovering and unravelling her story. There is pain and release in knowing that the clutter of her life will finally be free.

3. Exploring the elements

You do not need to experience a death to connect with the elements and their dance; you can do this in meditation. There is a formal meditation that can be engaged in, called the six-element practice in the Triratna Buddhist Order. This is generally taught to people as part of their ordination training, usually on their ordination course. It is best explored with spiritual friends in a structured context.

But there is scope to explore the elements mindfully as a means of loosening holding on. What follows is a brief overview of a guided meditation that helps you experience the elements directly.

1. To experience *space*, become aware of the area around you, the sounds, movements, and stimuli. They are around you, but also perceived within you.
2. To experience *consciousness*, become aware of the general tone of your inner experience – where does your attention go? Is your mind tight, vague, busy? Is it fast or slow? Watch it change, without wanting it to be otherwise.
3. To experience *earth*, become aware of the boundaries of your physical body, and be curious about any sense of support, stability, or heaviness and tightness. Again, experience without wanting it to be other than it is.
4. To experience *water*, notice the breath flowing in and out, just like waves coming up on the beach and then receding, or a ball rolling on a flat surface. Water is about flow. Is that movement gentle, forced, regular, relaxed?
5. To experience *fire*, open up to the subtle changes in temperature around you and in the breath itself as you breathe in and out.
6. To experience *air*, become aware of the expanding and retracting, the filling and emptying of the body as you breathe, the containing and releasing. Unlike water, the air element is three-dimensional – air moves in all directions.
7. Return and release back into the experience of the *space* around you.
8. Be present to how your *consciousness* has been affected by this exercise.

4. Return of the magician

By connecting to the elements, we return to the image of the magician explored in Chapter 1. In the image of the Tarot card described earlier, symbolic representations of four of the elements are placed before the Magician; the altar upon which they rest represents the space element. Without the altar, there is nowhere for the elements to manifest. Consciousness is possibly the presence of the Magician – or you, the viewer of the card.

By directly encountering the arising and passing of the elements, the ebb and flow, we approach the power of Buddhist ritual in its fullness: this is a rite of transformation and transmutation. And often, after the transference of merit verses have faded, a new sound, a new mantra, is chanted – the mantra of the archetypal teacher or magician.

The robust or the mournful Padmasambhava mantra is chanted to herald this radical transformation. This makes sense when you know the biography of this enigmatic figure. Like others of the protectors, Padmasambhava is a complex figure who blends myth, fact, symbol, and allegory into a dynamic form. He is the precious teacher, a tamer of demons, a wild magician, a compassionate friend. Guru Rimpoche is a maverick, yet simultaneously devoted to tradition. He is both a prince and a miraculously born child. Padmasambhava blends admonishment with joy, power with kindness, and the impossible with the possible.

And who is he? I would suggest sitting, as suggested earlier, with an image of Padmasambhava like this one, and allowing aspects of the imagery to invite you into his mysteries. Be curious without fixing on any ideas.

That said, these are some of my own thoughts on the image. His expression holds two contradictory expressions: is he stern and cheerful at the same time? His frown appears to be firmly pointing out our flaws with a hint of frustration, but the smile indicates he knows you understand and can trust that he has your best interests at heart. He is a firm, unrelenting friend who will not let you get away with things.

Padmasambhava carries a tantric staff with heads skewered on it, but, rather than being wielded ferociously, the weapon rests nonchalantly in the crook of his arm. It's just there in case it is needed. Padmasambhava is ever at the ready to decapitate our greed, hatred, and delusion.

His right hand delicately holds a vajra or diamond thunderbolt. The gesture of that hand points to his role as a tamer of demons, of negative forces and destructive tendencies. This is not a heavy metal 'Rock on!' gesture, but a sign to tame and redirect habits and energies that impede our spiritual progress. Is this implying that it takes a careful channelling of energies to transform unskilful habits? Padmasambhava's left hand gently cups a swirling potion topped with treasures and offerings. This potion is the amrita – the nectar of deathlessness. The receptacle itself is a clue – a human skull cup or kapala. Yet another brutal piece of death imagery! But, as we saw with Mahakala, a skull bowl represents something far more significant than a decapitated head. A kapala is a question and an answer in one – if you suffer and fear death, sacrifice your craving, fear, and even sense of identity. Die to holding on to being alive.

Padmasambhava also has curious feathers in his red lotus cap. Above the red petals turned up around the brim is a plume of vulture feathers. Vultures soar high in the blue sky with a minimum of effort. They whirl about freely above the mountains. They also consume carrion, and, in some regions of Tibet, are an important part of funerary practices. Freedom is possible, imply the feathers; you too can soar, but only if you fully realize and integrate the truth of impermanence.

The colours Padmasambhava wears suggest that he masters of all forms of Dharma, all expressions of the teachings, rather than being limited himself to just one path. Perhaps this points to the unity of all Dharmas. He literally wraps himself in the yellow of early Buddhism, the blue of the Mahayana, and the red of the Vajrayana. Padmasambhava is, after all, the Precious Teacher, the Guru Rimpoche who is unafraid to show you the truth you need in this moment.

Much more could be said about Padmasambhava's role as the archetypal teacher, but Sangharakshita communicates something of this protector when he writes personally about his first encounter with Padmasambhava while living in India. Padmasambhava is an old friend we may not have met as yet. He is the friend who shakes us up and sets us on the right path:

> Though I had never seen an image of Padmasambhava
> before, it was familiar to me in a way that no other figure
> on earth was familiar: familiar and fascinating. It was
> familiar as my own self, yet at the same time infinitely
> mysterious, infinitely wonderful, and inspiring it was to
> remain. Indeed, from then on the figure of the Precious
> Guru – Guru Rimpoche – was to occupy a permanent place
> in my inner spiritual world, even as it played a prominent
> part in the spiritual life and imagination of the entire
> Himalayan region.[72]

Perhaps only the great Vajra Guru who turned demons into protectors can ignite the transformation that is about to take place within us and point us in the direction of Enlightenment.

5. Concluding mantras

Once Padmasambhava's mercurial mantra fades, all that is left of us is... the protectors. We have been the protectors all along, or rather, will be, if we follow the Bodhisattva path as laid out in the puja. Of course, this is not going to happen during your first puja, unless your merit is particularly refined, but, should you take up puja as a spiritual practice in its own right, there is no end to where it might take you.

With the final mantras, we breathe the protectors into the present moment – or, to put it perhaps somewhat provocatively, it is them who breathe us into existence. Their qualities are part of our nature, hence we are able to understand and enact them. In a sense, the concluding mantras reflect our true nature, enlightened activity, which is no nature. Like the blue sky – which appears to have form but is empty of it – the protectors are perceived, but when investigated they are also empty. This is why such images, when visualized in various sadhana practices, are seen as insubstantial, non-solid beings of light. This is a great mystery that is worthy of exploration.[73]

The protectors are what lie at the end of the Mahayana view of Dharma practice – the figure of the Bodhisattva – so their mantras are a fitting conclusion to the puja. They represent and manifest the 'actual presence of Enlightenment [...] in the world and in our own being'.[74] By evoking their qualities, we can lose our limited selves in their august presence. Perhaps we might even bring some of their qualities with us as we leave the shrine room, don our shoes, and exit into the night?

Figure	One area of meaning...	Mantra
Avalokitesvara	Universal compassion for all beings in whatever state of existence	*om mani padme hum*
Manjusri	Radiant wisdom that cuts through ignorance and speaks the truth eloquently	*om a ra pa ca na dhih*
Vajrapani	Spiritual energy that breaks through obstacles	*om vajrapani hum*
Green Tara	Active compassion that saves from all sources of fear	*om tare tuttare ture svaha*
Amitabha	Infinite love and light, deep meditative contentment	*om amideva hrih*
Shakyamuni Buddha	The Buddha of our time	*om muni muni maha muni sakyamuni svaha*

Figure	One area of meaning...	Mantra
Padmasambhava	Spiritual transformation, robust truth telling, and ruthless love	*om ah hum vajra guru padma siddhi hum*
Prajnaparamita – *Heart Sutra*	Essence of wisdom, the appearance and absence of all phenomena	*gate gate paragate parasamgate bodhi svaha*

The ritual ends once these mantras and the final chant of *om shanti* (peace, peace, peace) has faded into the silence of the candlelit room.

There is nothing more to recite, to chant, to reflect upon. A profound stillness envelops you, an expectant hush. The world seems paused on an in-breath, or is it an out-breath? Resting is significant at this juncture. Buddhist rituals are incredibly active; our body, our voice, and our mind are constantly engaged, not to mention our emotions. At best, all these are united and oriented towards being of service to others. This is a big drain on our energies, though it can also invigorate us. Many people speak of being highly energized after puja, and struggle with sleeping straight afterwards, particularly if the ritual is conducted at night. So resting is an opportunity to let go and just be, giving yourself a break.

As well as being a chance to release any effort, this is also a precious opportunity to absorb the effects of the practice. Perhaps a new association or connection has been made through this most recent recitation of the *Heart Sutra*? Maybe your response to the Padmasambhava mantra has reminded you of a powerful moment of change, or evoked a memory? It could be that you are feeling emboldened or vulnerable, and need time to process the emotions. Whatever you are experiencing needs to be met, not shunted aside so you can return to the next item on the to-do list. This time of silence is a valuable opportunity to learn from the ritual process and allow that knowledge to be embedded deeply.

As the silence ends and the bells ring, this is your time to consider what you have just done. A puja is more than a piece of theatre, a cultural experience, or even a devotional practice – it is a reorientation of your life's direction and motivation. Yes, that's what it is, though only if engaged in with sincerity and awareness of the purpose. Knowing that, as you leave the silence and the shrine room, you could reflect on who you want to be, and how you want to act in order to live up to your potential.

This ritual ends. You pack up the cushions and get ready to return to the world. But this is where the next ritual starts, in the space between pujas – putting the words into practice.

6. The chapter in review

- Reflecting on and connecting to the six elements can help you gain insight into the contingent nature of all phenomena.
- Transformation is the life-blood of ritual.
- Puja is a journey or a story that leads you from one state to another.
- The concluding mantras are an opportunity to connect with aspects of humanity's highest potential through the mantras of key Buddhas and Bodhisattvas.
- Puja can be performed at any time, with any degree of simplicity or complexity.
- Silence at the end of a puja is an opportunity to rest, absorb, and then go forth into the world as a conduit for change.

Conclusion

We have journeyed a long way over the course of this book, approaching Enlightenment. We began with seeing the world and acting in it as a magician might – with knowledge, curiosity, and skill. Ritual is magic, but not in a limited or shallow sense. It also has a long tradition – and one that might seem inconvenient to the extent that it does not match a scientific world view. From this vantage point, we began with the understanding that to some degree we are trapped, confined by habit, entertained by superficiality, and confused by vagueness. There are three main ways we are held back from making progress towards Enlightenment.

The Sevenfold Puja or seven-limbed prayer begins by sawing vigorously at the shackle of superficiality by bringing our whole self present into the shrine room. Our body, speech, and mind are directed at the Buddha, his teachings and to the community of practitioners. We begin by saluting the shrine with a bow of grateful humility. Then, we adorn the shrine and all it represents with gifts as a recognition of our commitment ('Worship'). It is an investment, an act of generosity saying that the Three Refuges are worth more than anything else; even more than flowers, food, jewels, and entertainment. But these gifts are not just for the Buddha: they are for all beings. Here the insight begins to dawn, for we understand, even if only for a second, that all beings have the potential for Buddhahood, and thus, by association, all deserve to be treated as honoured guests.

In bowing to the shrine ('Salutation'), we are effectively meeting the Buddha at our door and welcoming him into our experience. In a sense, we are also awakening him in ourselves. Then we go for refuge; we are taking that commitment further by acknowledging that, as we intimated earlier, the Three Jewels are what matters most to us ('Going for refuge'). There is even less of the fetters of superficiality and vagueness holding us back now. The chains are developing cracks.

At this point we realize, in the spirit of honesty and revelation, that we have aspirations but do not always live up to them. We have committed acts that are shameful, so we face up to that rather than mire ourselves in a self-harm spiral of guilt. We commit to challenging these unskilful habits, and vow to break those dangerous patterns ('Confession of faults'). Again, we are also digging below the surface and fighting against that binding of superficiality.

In rejoicing, we have an opportunity to reflect that, yes, we have shadows, but we also contain light. In fact, so do a great many if not all beings. There are exemplars who can serve as lights in the darkness ('Rejoicing in merit'). Perhaps this challenges a pessimistic view and opens us up emotionally to others. Thus opened, we acknowledge that others have walked this path before us and have wisdom to offer. Could they make this advice available so that everyone, not just us, may make progress? We entreat them for guidance ('Entreaty and supplication'), so that the teachings remain vibrant forces in our lives and in the lives of others.

Along the way, we have voices raised in mantra. If Avalokitesvara is evoked with *om mani padme hum*, we are being asked to consider that all beings are in a similar predicament, though the intensity of their suffering may vary depending on circumstance. Some appear to be born blessed with good conditions, others in states of suffering. The mantra invites us to consider the possibility of working for the good of everyone, regardless of our likes and dislikes. Padmasambhava's mantra arrives to give us the energy to go forth into the world and be the change that is needed – acting with inspiration from the host of Buddha and Bodhisattva forms ('Dedication').

And then we surrender, we release any hope of reward, and we rest. Peace is evoked in the silence that marks the end, and also the beginning of the path. The beginning of the next ritual.

And so, we step ever closer to Enlightenment – one bow, one offering, one courageous acknowledgement at a time.

Appendix

The Sevenfold Puja

Namo buddhaya
Namo dharmaya
Namo sanghaya
Namo nama
om
ah
hum

I. Worship

With mandarava, blue lotus, and jasmine,
With all flowers pleasing and fragrant,
And with garlands skilfully woven,
I pay honour to the princes of the Sages,
So worthy of veneration.

I envelop them in clouds of incense,
Sweet and penetrating;
I make them offerings of food, hard and soft,
And pleasing kinds of liquids to drink.
I offer them lamps, encrusted with jewels,
Festooned with golden lotus.
On the paving, sprinkled with perfume,
I scatter handfuls of beautiful flowers.

II. Salutation

As many atoms as there are
In the thousand million worlds,
So many times I make reverent salutation
To all the Buddhas of the Three Eras,
To the Saddharma,
And to the excellent Community.

I pay homage to all the shrines,
And places in which the Bodhisattvas have been.
I make profound obeisance to the Teachers,
And those to whom respectful salutation is due.

III. Going for refuge

This very day
I go for my refuge
To the powerful protectors,
Whose purpose is to guard the universe;
The mighty conquerors who overcome suffering everywhere.

Wholeheartedly also I take my refuge
In the Dharma they have ascertained,
Which is the abode of security against the rounds of rebirth.
Likewise in the host of Bodhisattvas
I take my refuge.

The Three Refuges

Namo tassa bhagavato arahato sammasambuddhassa
Namo tassa bhagavato arahato sammasambuddhassa
Namo tassa bhagavato arahato sammasambuddhassa

Buddham saranam gacchami
Dhammam saranam gacchami
Sangham saranam gacchami

Dutiyampi buddham saranam gacchami

Dutiyampi dhammam saranam gacchami
Dutiyampi sangham saranam gacchami

Tatiyampi buddham saranam gacchami
Tatiyampi dhammam saranam gacchami
Tatiyampi sangham saranam gacchami

Translation

Homage to Him, the Blessed One, the Worthy One,
    the Perfectly Enlightened One!
To the Buddha for refuge I go.
To the Dharma for refuge I go.
To the Sangha for refuge I go.

For the second time to the Buddha for refuge I go.
For the second time to the Dharma for refuge I go.
For the second time to the Sangha for refuge I go.

For the third time to the Buddha for refuge I go.
For the third time to the Dharma for refuge I go.
For the third time to the Sangha for refuge I go.

The five precepts

Panatipata veramani-sikkhapadam samadiyami
Adinnadana veramani-sikkhapadam samadiyami
Kamesu micchacara veramani-sikkhapadam samadiyami
Musavada veramani-sikkhapadam samadiyami
Surameraya majja pamadatthana veramani-sikkhapadam samadiyami

Sadhu sadhu sadhu

The positive precepts

With deeds of loving kindness, I purify my body.
With open-handed generosity, I purify my body.
With stillness, simplicity, and contentment, I purify my body.
With truthful communication, I purify my speech.
With mindfulness clear and radiant, I purify my mind.

Translation

I undertake to abstain from taking life.
I undertake to abstain from taking the not-given.
I undertake to abstain from sexual misconduct.
I undertake to abstain from false speech.
I undertake to abstain from taking intoxicants.

Dharmacari / dharmacarini precepts

Panatipata veramani-sikkhapadam samadiyami
Adinnadana veramani-sikkhapadam samadiyami
Kamesu micchacara veramani-sikkhapadam samadiyami
Musavada veramani-sikkhapadam samadiyami
Pharusavacaya veramani-sikkhapadam samadiyami
Samphappalapa veramani-sikkhapadam samadiyami
Pisunavacaya veramani-sikkhapadam samadiyami
Abhijjhaya veramani-sikkhapadam samadiyami
Byapada veramani-sikkhapadam samadiyami
Micchaditthiya veramani-sikkhapadam samadiyami

Sadhu sadhu sadhu

The positive precepts

With deeds of loving kindness, I purify my body.
With open-handed generosity, I purify my body.
With stillness, simplicity, and contentment, I purify my body.
With truthful communication, I purify my speech.
With kindly communication, I purify my speech.
With helpful communication, I purify my speech.
With harmonious communication, I purify my speech.
Abandoning covetousness for tranquillity, I purify my mind.
Changing hatred into compassion, I purify my mind.
Transforming ignorance into wisdom, I purify my mind.

Translation

I undertake to abstain from taking life.
I undertake to abstain from taking the not-given.
I undertake to abstain from sexual misconduct.
I undertake to abstain from false speech.
I undertake to abstain from harsh speech.
I undertake to abstain from useless speech.
I undertake to abstain from slanderous speech.
I undertake to abstain from covetousness.
I undertake to abstain from animosity.
I undertake to abstain from false views.

IV. Confession of faults

The evil that I have heaped up
Through my ignorance and foolishness –
Evil in the world of everyday experience,
As well as evil in understanding and intelligence –
All that I acknowledge to the Protectors.

Standing before them
With hands raised in reverence,
And terrified of suffering,
I pay salutations again and again.

May the Leaders receive this kindly,
Just as it is, with its many faults!
What is not good, O Protectors,
I shall not do again.

V. Rejoicing in merit

I rejoice with delight
In the good done by all beings,
Through which they obtain rest
With the end of suffering.
May those who have suffered be happy!

I rejoice in the release of beings
From the sufferings of the rounds of existence;
I rejoice in the nature of the Bodhisattva
And the Buddha,
Who are Protectors.

I rejoice in the arising of the Will to Enlightenment,
And the Teaching:
Those Oceans that bring happiness to all beings,
And are the abode of welfare of all beings.

VI. Entreaty and supplication

Saluting them with folded hands
I entreat the Buddhas in all the quarters:
May they make shine the lamp of the Dharma
For those wandering in the suffering of delusion!

With hands folded in reverence
I implore the conquerors desiring to enter Nirvana:
May they remain here for endless ages,
So that life in this world does not grow dark.

The *Heart Sutra*

The Bodhisattva of Compassion,
When he meditated deeply,
Saw the emptiness of all five skandhas
And sundered the bonds that caused him suffering.

Here then,
Form is no other than emptiness,
Emptiness no other than form.
Form is only emptiness,
Emptiness only form.

Feeling, thought, and choice,
Consciousness itself,
Are the same as this.

All things are by nature void,
They are not born or destroyed;
Nor are they stained or pure,
Nor do they wax or wane.

So, in emptiness, no form,
No feeling, thought, or choice,
Nor is there consciousness.

No eye, ear, nose, tongue, body, mind;
No colour, sound, smell, taste, touch,
Or what the mind takes hold of,
Nor even act of sensing.

No ignorance or end of it,
Nor all that comes of ignorance;
No withering, no death,
No end of them.

Nor is there pain, or cause of pain,
Or cease in pain, or noble path
To lead from pain;
Not even wisdom to attain!
Attainment too is emptiness.

So know that the Bodhisattva
Holding to nothing whatever,
But dwelling in Prajna wisdom,
Is freed of delusive hindrance,
Rid of the fear bred by it,
And reaches clearest Nirvana.

All Buddhas of past and present,
Buddhas of future time,
Using this Prajna wisdom,
Come to full and perfect vision.

Hear then the great dharani,
The radiant peerless mantra,
The Prajnaparamita

Whose words allay all pain;
Hear and believe its truth!

Gate gate paragate parasamgate bodhi svaha

VII. Transference of merit and self-surrender

May the merit gained
In my acting thus
Go to the alleviation of the suffering of all beings.
My personality throughout my existences,
My possessions,
And my merit in all three ways,
I give up without regard to myself
For the benefit of all beings.

Just as the earth and other elements
Are serviceable in many ways
To the infinite number of beings
Inhabiting limitless space;
So may I become
That which maintains all beings
Situated throughout space,
So long as all have not attained
To peace.[75]

Illustration Credits

Page 13 Illustration of the Magician card from A. E. Waite, *The Pictorial Key to the Tarot*, William Rider & Son, London 1911. Artist: Pamela Colman Smith.

Page 16 Simple depiction of the ouroboros symbol by AnonMoos, 2009. https://upload.wikimedia.org/wikipedia/commons/c/c8/Ouroboros-simple.svg. Public domain.

Pages 58 & 59 Scott McCloud, *Understanding Comics: The Invisible Art*, HarperCollins, New York 1993, pp.24–5.

Page 66 Meditating Buddha, Pakistan, ca. third to fifth century CE, Metropolitan Museum of Art, New York, accession number 1984.486.6. Met Open Access.

Page 110 Adaptation of the Avalokitesvara mantra indicating syllable colours in Tibetan script, originally by Christopher J. Fynn. Creative Commons.

Page 116 Shadakshari Avalokiteshvara, Tibetan (Artist), late 12th–13th century, tempera on cloth (India, Nepal, and Tibet). Creative Commons.

Page 139 Six-armed Mahakala owned and photographed by the author, painted by unknown Tibetan refugee artist.

Page 186 Padmasambhava, painting by Dharmachari Chintamani.

Notes

Prologue

1 *The Complete Works of Sangharakshita*, vol.18: *Milarepa and the Art of Discipleship I*, ed. Vidyadevi, Windhorse Publications, Cambridge 2018, p.168.

Chapter one

2 Subhuti and Sangharakshita, 'Reimagining the Buddha', *Seven Papers* (revised December 2018), available at https://thebuddhistcentre. com/system/files/groups/files/seven_papers_by_subhuti_with_ sangharakshita_-_version_2_with_index.pdf, accessed on 28 February 2024, p.73.

3 Chris Gosden, *The History of Magic*, Viking, London 2020, p.9.

4 Janet and Anne Grahame Johnstone, *A Book of Children's Names*, Dean & Sons, London 1969, p.18.

5 Ursula K. Le Guin, *A Wizard of Earthsea*, Gollancz, London 2018, p.28.

6 Asvaghosa, *Buddhacarita*, ch.16, available at http://www.khandro. net/Acts_of_the_Buddha_toc.htm, accessed on 28 February 2024.

7 Sangharakshita, *The Bodhisattva Ideal*, Windhorse Publications, Birmingham 1999, p.134.

8 See https://quiabsurdum.com/glossary/oroboros/, accessed on 28 February 2024.

Chapter two

9 *Sundarika-Bharadvaja Sutta* from the *Sutta Nipata*, trans. Bhikkhu Sujato, available at https://suttacentral.net/snp3.4/en/ sujato?layout=plain&reference=none&notes=asterisk&highlight= false&script=latin, accessed on 4 March 2024.

10 For those interested in the rich tradition of Buddhist magic that is concerned with manifesting control over the external world or in importuning deities, I would recommend *Buddhist Magic: Divination, Healing, and Enchantment through the Ages* by Sam Van Schaik, Shambhala, Boulder, CO, 2020. This book examines evidence from sources found along the Silk Road that suggest there was a trade in spells, potions, and artefacts that blended Buddhist, Vedic, and other ideas into a system of spell casting.

11 *Sigalovada Sutta* from the *Digha Nikaya*, trans. Narada Thera, available at https://www.accesstoinsight.org/tipitaka/dn/dn.31.0.nara.html, accessed on 4 March 2024.

12 Finding the origins of this axiom is complicated. Anaïs Nin in her novel *Seduction of the Minotaur* (1964) has one of her characters reference the Talmud, an ancient Hebrew text, as the source of this quotation. The closest match comes from a section of the Talmud called Berakoth 55b, which is concerned with the origins of dreams rather than the nature of perception. The nearest quote is: 'A man is shown in a dream only what is suggested by his own thoughts.' See https://halakhah.com/berakoth/berakoth_55.html#PARTb, accessed on 4 March 2024.

13 Donald S. Lopez, Jr, *The Scientific Buddha: His Short and Happy Life*, Yale University Press, New Haven, CT, 2012, pp.38–9.

14 Dimitris Xygalatas, *Ritual: How Seemingly Senseless Acts Make Life Worth Living*, Profile Books, London 2022.

15 Xygalatas, *Ritual*, p.88.

16 Erich Fromm, quoted by Sangharakshita in *Ritual and Devotion in Buddhism: An Introduction*, Windhorse Publications, Birmingham 1999, p.29.

17 Erich Fromm, *To Have or To Be?*, Abacus, New York 1976, p.135.

18 The *Avatamsaka Sutra* or *Flower Ornament Scripture* exists in many translations. Thomas Cleary's translation published by Shambhala in 1993 is readily available in print and online. You can read it at https://terebess.hu/english/Flower-Ornament.pdf, accessed on 4 March 2024.

19 'The king of aspiration prayers: Samantabhadra's "Aspiration to good actions"', available at https://www.lotsawahouse.org/words-of-the-buddha/samantabhadra-aspiration-good-actions, accessed on 4 March 2024.

20 Atisha, *Lamp for the Path to Enlightenment*, trans. Ruth Sonam, Snow Lion Publications, New York 1997, p.152.

Chapter three

21 Charles Dickens, *A Christmas Carol,* Project Gutenberg online edition, Stave One, https://www.gutenberg.org/cache/epub/19337/pg19337-images.html, accessed on 10 February 2023.

22 Sangharakshita, *The Taste of Freedom*, Windhorse Publications, Birmingham 1997, pp.19–22.

23 Sangharakshita, *The Taste of Freedom*, p.22.

Chapter four

24 Le Guin, *A Wizard of Earthsea*, p.17.

25 Semiotics is the investigation of how meaning is constructed by the interplay between signs and symbols. This discipline explores both verbal and non-verbal signs and the cultural loading given to them.

26 Scott McCloud, *Understanding Comics: The Invisible Art*, HarperCollins, New York 1993.

27 *Kawaii* is a contemporary Japanese term that means 'cute' or 'adorable'. It is a specific aesthetic celebrated in Japanese pop culture, but also admired around the world. The *kawaii* aesthetic presents images of animals, people, and inanimate objects rendered with a child-like innocence in a style that could be considered cartoonish. These lovable characters, found in comic books, toys, and fashion, are admired by young and old alike.

28 René Magritte was a surrealist artist from Belgium who rose to fame during his time painting in Paris during the 1920s. His work, influenced by his training as a graphic artist, mostly avoided abstract shapes and used more figurative forms. In his paintings, recognizable mundane objects such as fruit, hats, pipes, and blue skies laced with clouds are infused with surreal dimensions.

29 The Tibetan teachings on outer, inner, secret, and ultimate levels of meaning come to us from the Dzogchen tradition, otherwise known as the 'Great Perfection' or 'Great Completeness'. The Dzogchen teachings are arranged in three collections. The third, called *Mengakdé*, arranges Buddhist texts based on the capacities and inclinations of practitioners. These four categories are in a sequence moving from the external expression of practice through to full realization. The four levels are applied in many areas of practice, whether it is concerned with levels of refuge or the making of offerings. Sources for the levels are available at https://www.lotsawahouse.org/tibetan-masters/shechen-gyaltsab/explanation-of-generation-stage-for-beginners, accessed on 5 March 2024. The framework is implied within the Triratna Buddhist Order's levels of going for refuge. See https://www.freebuddhistaudio.com/texts/read?num=137, accessed on 5 March 2024.

30 See *The History of My Going for Refuge*, ch.18, in *The Complete Works of Sangharakshita*, vol.2: *The Three Jewels I*, ed. Kalyanaprabha, Windhorse Publications, Cambridge 2019, pp.479–83.

31 The Bimaran Reliquary, Afghanistan, ca. first century CE, on display at the British Museum, London; image available at https://www.britishmuseum.org/collection/object/A_1900-0209-1, accessed on 5 March 2024.

32 There are any number of reputable podcasts that explore the Buddha's life and teaching. Free Buddhist Audio is one such invaluable resource: see https://www.freebuddhistaudio.com/, accessed on 5 March 2024.

Chapter five

33 Sangharakshita, *Milarepa and the Art of Discipleship I*, p.619.

34 Robert Beer, *The Encyclopedia of Tibetan Symbols and Motifs*, Shambhala, Boston 1999, p.154. This gesture is of the hands cupped lightly, not pressed together as in Christian prayer. It is symbolic of a

lotus flower. The thumbs touching and creating an open oval shape is suggestive of the Bodhicitta resting in the heart of the lotus.

35 A guided version of this technique is available at Yongey Mingyur Rinpoche, 'Essence of all mantras: vajra recitation', available at https://www.youtube.com/watch?v=WaAbelZnEtM, accessed 29 December 2021.

36 Sangharakshita, *Seminar notes on The Meeting at Silver Spring*, Padmaloka Retreat Centre, Norwich 1976, p.12.

37 Lama Anagarika Govinda, *Foundations of Tibetan Mysticism*, Weiser Books, Boston 1969, p.22.

38 Lama Anagarika Govinda, *Creative Meditation and Multi-Dimensional Consciousness*, Quest Books, Illinois 1976, p. 72.

39 Govinda, *Foundations*, p.131.

Chapter six

40 Sangharakshita, *Creative Symbols of Tantric Buddhism*, Windhorse Publications, Birmingham 2002, p.141.

41 The Threefold Puja in English is available at https://thebuddhistcentre.com/system/files/groups/files/threefoldpuja.pdf, accessed on 6 March 2024. It is available in other languages at https://thebuddhistcentre.com/search/node/%22threefold%20puja%22%20%22threefold%20puja%22, accessed on 6 March 2024.

42 Sangharakshita, *Ritual and Devotion*, p.44.

43 For more on the noble eightfold path, I would recommend Sangharakshita's book *Vision and Transformation: An Introduction to the Buddha's Noble Eightfold Path*, 2nd ed., Windhorse Publications, Birmingham 1999.

44 Sangharakshita, *Creative Symbols*, pp.133–57.

45 From *Puja: The Triratna Book of Buddhist Devotional Texts*, Windhorse Publications, Cambridge 2022.

Chapter seven

46 Sangharakshita, *What Is the Dharma? The Essential Teachings of the Buddha*, Windhorse Publications, Birmingham 1998, pp.146–8.

47 See https://www.etymonline.com/word/compassion, accessed on 9 March 2024.

48 Jayarava, 'Visible mantra', available at https://www.visiblemantra.org/, accessed on 6 March 2024.

49 Sangharakshita, *Creative Symbols*, p.168.

Chapter eight

50 *A Dhammapada for Contemplation*, trans. Ajahn Munindo, available at https://www.abhayagiri.org/books/614-a-dhammapada-for-contemplation, accessed on 7 March 2024, verses 188–92.

51 *Samannaphala Sutta: The Fruits of the Homeless Life*, in *The Long Discourses of the Buddha: A Translation of the Digha Nikaya*, trans. Maurice Walshe, Wisdom Publications, Boston 1995, p.108.

52 'Punnika and the Brahman' from the *Therigatha*, available at https:/
/www.accesstoinsight.org/tipitaka/kn/thig/thig.12.01.than.html,
accessed on 7 March 2024.

53 Sangharakshita, *The Ten Pillars of Buddhism*, Windhorse Publications,
Birmingham 2004, p.21.

54 The five Buddhas or jinas (conquerors) reflect different facets
of Enlightenment with which we might connect. Unlike the
historical Buddha, these Buddhas are not bound by the confines
of time – rather they occupy a mythic, archetypal realm. As with
Avalokitesvara, they can be seen as anthropomorphic embodiments
of core Buddhist values and practices.

55 *Sutra of Forty-Two Sections*, available at https://huntingtonarchive.
org/resources/downloads/sutras/01earlyTexts/The%20Sutra%20
of%2042%20Sections.pdf, accessed on 7 March 2024.

56 For more on this topic, I would recommend Nagapriya's thorough
exploration in *Exploring Karma and Rebirth*, Windhorse Publications,
Birmingham 2004.

57 See the Threefold Puja from *Puja: The Triratna Book of Buddhist
Devotional Texts*, pp.33–5.

Chapter nine

58 Sangharakshita, *Living Ethically*, Windhorse Publications, Cambridge
2009, p.172.

59 Oscar Wilde, *The Picture of Dorian Gray*, available at https://www.
gutenberg.org/files/174/174-h/174-h.htm, accessed on 7 March
2024, ch.7.

60 *Dhammapada*, verse 165.

Chapter ten

61 Sangharakshita, *The Bodhisattva Ideal*, p.51.

62 Paul Rozin and Edward B. Royzman, 'Negativity bias, negativity
dominance, and contagion', *Personality and Social Psychology
Review* 5:4, 2001, pp.296–320, available at https://www.
behaviorismandmentalhealth.com/wp-content/uploads/2022/
03/Negativity_Bias_Negativity_Dominance_and_Contagion.pdf,
accessed on 9 March 2024.

Chapter eleven

63 *Dhammapada*, verse 100.

64 Jayarava Attwood, 'Losing ourselves in the *Heart Sutra*', *Tricycle
Magazine*, spring 2021, available at https://tricycle.org/magazine/
heart-sutra-history/, accessed on 8 March 2024.

65 Sangharakshita, *The Eternal Legacy: An Introduction to the Canonical
Literature of Buddhism*, Windhorse Publications, Birmingham 2006.

66 Harvard Graduate School of Education, 'Project Zero's thinking
routine toolbox', available at https://pz.harvard.edu/thinking-
routines, accessed on 8 March 2024.

Chapter twelve

67 Susannah Clarke, *Jonathan Strange & Mr Norrell*, Bloomsbury, New York 2004, p.160.
68 Empedocles, *Poem on natural philosophy*, trans. Nicolaas van der Ben, available at https://www.academia.edu/40459174/Empedocles_Poem_on_natural_philosophy/, accessed on 11 March 2024, p.87.
69 *Dhatu-vibhanga Sutta: An Analysis of the Properties* from the *Majjhima Nikaya*, trans. Thanissaro Bhikkhu, available at https://www.accesstoinsight.org/tipitaka/mn/mn.140.than.html, accessed on 11 March 2024.
70 *Maha-Rahulovada Sutta: The Greater Exhortation to Rahula* from the *Majjhima Nikaya*, trans. Thanissaro Bhikkhu, available at https://www.accesstoinsight.org/tipitaka/mn/mn.062.than.html, accessed on 11 March 2024.
71 Sangharakshita, *The Three Jewels: The Central Ideals of Buddhism*, Windhorse Publications, Birmingham 1998, p.89.
72 Sangharakshita, *Facing Mount Kanchenjunga: An English Buddhist on the Eastern Himalayas*, Windhorse Publications, Glasgow 1991, p.100.
73 For a thorough introduction to these Buddhist protectors and more, see Vessantara's impressive book *Meeting the Buddhas: A Guide to Buddhas, Bodhisattvas, and Tantric Deities*, Windhorse Publications, Cambridge 2022.
74 Sangharakshita, *Ritual and Devotion*, p.113.

Appendix

75 The Sevenfold Puja from *Puja: The Triratna Book of Buddhist Devotional Texts*, pp.7–29.

Index

Introductory Note

References such as '178–9' indicate (not necessarily continuous) discussion of a topic across a range of pages. Wherever possible in the case of topics with many references, these have either been divided into sub-topics or only the most significant discussions of the topic are listed. Because the entire work is about 'Enlightenment', the use of this term (and certain others which occur constantly throughout the book) as an entry point has been restricted. Information will be found under the corresponding detailed topics.

Padmasambhava 186–8, 190, 194
pain 41–2, 105–6, 108, 111–13, 127, 152, 155, 201–2
paintings 36, 60–1, 140, 142, 174
Pakistan 66, 170
Pali 33, 39, 119, 125, 129–31, 135
passions 13, 81, 125, 140
paths 36, 47, 64–5, 67–9, 94–6, 118–19, 158–9, 166–7
  Bodhisattva 168, 188
  noble 96, 201
  right 64, 188
  spiritual 24, 67, 165
patience 17, 53, 55, 57, 76, 103, 111–12, 141
peace 23, 79, 81, 179, 190, 194, 202
perceptions 28, 42–3, 51, 63, 81, 86, 131
perfections 9, 111–13, 115, 141
persistence 69, 116, 160
personality 179, 202
phenomena 11, 14, 79–81, 83, 86, 96, 169, 190–1
phenomenal world 13–14, 64, 181–2
philosopher 26–7, 181
philosophy 28
physical body 80–1, 133, 185
places, sacred 73–4, 123
poems 126, 181; see also verses
positive precepts 135, 197–8
possessions 14, 69, 141, 179, 202
postures 67, 70, 74, 88
potions 6, 8, 187
power xviii, xx–1, 7–9, 47–8, 60–1, 82–4, 145–6, 186
practice
  levels of 63, 78
  of mantra 107, 109–10
  regular 94, 103, 120, 161
  seven-limbed xix, 34–5
  spiritual 8, 23, 39, 55, 63, 107, 188
practitioners 6, 9, 24–5, 34, 36, 75–8, 102, 145–6
praise/praising 39, 83, 94, 160–1, 163
Prajnaparamita 190, 201
prayer 22–3, 35–6, 39

seven-limbed 34–5, 39, 47, 102, 193
precepts 135–7, 140, 157, 159
  body 129–30
  dharmacarini 198
  five 128–9, 148, 197
  mind 131–2
  positive 135, 197–8
  and refuges 127–32, 135
  speech 130–1
preliminaries 35–6, 39
pride 11, 38, 77, 111
progress, spiritual 36, 42, 78, 187
Project Zero 172
prostration 34, 39, 50, 77
  full-body 50, 78, 162
protectors 132, 137, 145–6, 156–7, 186, 188–9, 196, 199–200
psychology 8, 26, 83, 143
puja 33–5, 37, 93–4, 96–7, 102–4, 155–8, 167–9, 188–91
  Sevenfold 34–5, 37, 39, 102, 115, 117, 193, 195
  Threefold 93–8, 103, 120, 135
purity 79–81, 144

Rahula 182–3
reading xix, 7, 18, 56–8, 66, 146, 168–70
  and entreaty 175–6
  things to try 176–7
realms 110–11, 113–14, 121, 134, 147, 152, 155, 160
realms of existence 111, 134, 136, 160
rebirth, rounds of 132–4, 196
receptivity 81, 109, 117
recitation 109, 116, 137, 190
refuge 36–7, 39, 93, 123–36, 145, 157, 193–4, 196–7
  going for, see going for refuge
  refuges and precepts 127–32, 135
  things to try 135–6
  true 123–4
regular practice 94, 103, 120, 161
rejoicing 39, 151–63, 194
  in merit 34, 149, 155–7, 162, 199
  and negativity 151–5, 162

Tibetan 12, 82, 84, 98–9, 102, 176
traffic islands 124, 133
transactional relationships 22–3, 94
transference of merit 149, 202
transformation 8, 12, 27, 117, 186,
188, 191
treasures 33, 82, 170, 187
trees 3, 49, 147
trials 7, 12, 77
Triratna Buddhist Community xix,
19, 34, 93, 120
Triratna Buddhist Order xix, 43,
128, 184
Triratna Buddhist tradition 34, 99,
160
truth 19–20, 61, 95–6, 131, 134,
142–3, 155–6, 187–9
universal 19, 79, 129
truthful communication 130, 135,
197–8

ultimate meaning 64, 100–1
understanding 8–9, 61, 63, 79, 81,
96, 100–1, 129–32
uninformed mind 176
unity 15, 136, 182, 188
universal compassion 115, 118, 140,
145, 148, 189
universal truth 19, 79, 129
universe 3–4, 24, 80, 132, 145–6,
196
universities 27, 30, 56
unskilful actions 145–6, 150, 180
untruths 131

vagueness 45–6, 53, 174, 193–4
fetter of 45
vajra 15, 62–4, 187
breathing 78, 88, 103
Vajrapani 84, 189
Vajrayana 63, 188

values 32–3, 37, 76, 105, 109, 154,
157, 160
shared 31–2, 74, 105, 128
verses 33–5, 93–4, 103, 115, 118–20,
149, 156, 180–1
entreaty and supplication 167–8
protective 106–10
views
how to view 49–51
and rituals 46–9
things to try 51–2
voices 60, 115–16, 125, 160, 162–3,
168, 190, 194

walls xvii, 92, 138
wands 6, 14–15
water 6, 10, 44–5, 78, 98–100, 102,
181–3, 185
waves 43–5, 92, 185
weapons 2, 9, 63, 187
welfare 23, 80, 128, 156–7, 200
wellbeing 105, 121
Western symbolism 13–14, 20
wheel 34, 43, 110, 134, 153, 155, 160
Wilde, Oscar 140
wind 6, 119, 181–2
wisdom 8, 11, 14, 111, 113, 141, 145,
148
wizards 4–5, 7
wooden fish 76, 93, 124
word/outer meaning 62, 100–1
worship 33, 36, 91–104, 119, 193,
195
ten thousand Buddhas not
enough 91–3
things to try 103–4
three offerings 93–6

Xygalatas, Dimitris 30–2, 74

Yoda (character) 6, 14

WINDHORSE PUBLICATIONS

Windhorse Publications is a Buddhist charitable company based in the UK. Our books, which are distributed internationally, champion Buddhism, meditation, and mindfulness. They offer fresh interpretations of Buddhist teachings and their application to contemporary life, with subject matter and authors from across the Buddhist tradition, catering for a broad range of interest and experience. In addition to publishing titles exploring classic texts for modern audiences, we aspire to publish books that offer a Buddhist perspective on today's challenges, including social inequality, the environment and climate, gender, mental health, and more. Established in the 1970s to publish the writing of Urgyen Sangharakshita (1925–2018), the founder of the Triratna Buddhist Order, Windhorse Publications continues to be dedicated to preserving and keeping in print his impressive and influential body of work, making it accessible for future generations. As well as high quality print and eBooks, Windhorse Publications produces accompanying audio, podcast, video, and teaching resources.

Windhorse Publications
38 Newmarket Road
Cambridge CB5 8DT
info@windhorsepublications.com

North America Distributors: Consortium Book Sales & Distribution
210 American Drive
Jackson TN 38301
USA
www.cbsd.com

Australia and New Zealand Distributors: Windhorse Books
PO Box 574
Newtown NSW 2042
Australia
windhorse.com.au/books.html

THE TRIRATNA BUDDHIST COMMUNITY

Windhorse Publications is a part of the Triratna Buddhist Community, an international movement with centres in Europe, India, North and South America, and Australasia. At these centres, members of the Triratna Buddhist Order offer classes in meditation and Buddhism. Activities of the Triratna Community also include retreat centres, residential spiritual communities, ethical Right Livelihood businesses, and the Karuna Trust, a UK fundraising charity that supports social welfare projects in the slums and villages of India.

Through these and other activities, Triratna is developing a unique approach to Buddhism, not simply as a philosophy and a set of techniques, but as a creatively directed way of life for all people living in the conditions of the modern world.

If you would like more information about Triratna please visit thebuddhistcentre.com or write to:

London Buddhist Centre
51 Roman Road
London E2 0HU
UK
contact@lbc.org.uk

Aryaloka
14 Heartwood Circle
Newmarket NH 03857
USA
info@aryaloka.org

Sydney Buddhist Centre
24 Enmore Road
Sydney NSW 2042
Australia
info@sydneybuddhistcentre.org.au

Not About Being Good
A Practical Guide to Buddhist Ethics
Subhadramati

While there are numerous books on Buddhist meditation and philosophy, there are few books that are entirely devoted to the practice of Buddhist ethics. Subhadramati communicates clearly both their founding principles and the practical methods to embody them.

Buddhist ethics are not about conforming to a set of conventions, not about 'being good' in order to gain rewards. Instead, living ethically springs from the awareness that other people are no different from yourself. You can actively develop this awareness, through cultivating love, clarity and contentment. Helping you to come into greater harmony with all that lives, this is ultimately your guidebook to a more satisfactory life.

'In touch with the wonder of being alive, Subhadramati is a realistic and sympathetic guide to ethics in the twenty-first century.' – Vidyamala Burch, author of *Mindfulness for Health*

'Writing with passion, humour and delicacy, gloriously free from moralism, her aim is to help us live a richer and fuller life.' – Maitreyabandhu, author of *Life with Full Attention*

'Places ethics and meditation at the heart of Buddhist practice, and shows how they work together in transforming ordinary human beings into Buddhas.' – Professor Damien Keown, author of *The Nature of Buddhist Ethics*

1SBN 9781 909314 01 6
176 pages

Life with Full Attention
A Practical Course in Mindfulness
Maitreyabandhu

In this eight-week course on mindfulness, Maitreyabandhu teaches you how to pay closer attention to experience. Each week he introduces a different aspect of mindfulness – such as awareness of the body, feelings, thoughts and the environment – and recommends a number of easy practices; from trying out a simple meditation to reading a poem. Featuring personal stories, examples and suggestions, *Life with Full Attention* is a valuable aid to mindfulness both as a starting point and for the more experienced.

ISBN 9781 899579 98 3
328 pages

It's Not Out There
How to See Differently and Live an Extraordinary, Ordinary Life
Danapriya

Most of us constantly look outside ourselves for something: happiness, love, contentment. But this something is not out there. 'It' is within us. We are full of these qualities: happiness, love, contentment and more.

In *It's Not Out There*, Buddhist teacher and mentor, Danapriya, helps you to look inside yourself in such a way that life becomes more vivid, joyful and extraordinary.

If you want to suffer less and to live life more fully, this book is for you. It's about seeing the reality of the human predicament, and seeing through the illusions that create unnecessary pain for yourself and others. This book uncovers the fertile ground of your own potential, and enables you to live the life you are here for. Stop, look, listen and sense, you are worth it.

'Written in simple, down-to-earth language, It's Not Out There *is brimming with practical wisdom. Positive and encouraging, Danapriya shares ways to help anyone who wants to change their life and find greater happiness and fulfilment.'* – Dr Paramabandhu Groves, co-author of *Eight Step Recovery: Using the Buddha's Teachings to Overcome Addiction*

'Reading this book is like having a conversation with a wise friend – someone who doesn't just talk at you but who is interested in your thoughts and experience too. Buy one for everyone you know who is serious about life and how to live it well.' – Subhadramati, author of *Not About Being Good*

Born Ian Dixon in 1959, Danapriya ('one who loves giving') has been involved in personal growth and healing work for over three decades. Ordained into the Triratna Buddhist Order in 2001, he founded the Deal Buddhist Group in Kent, UK, in 2007. Based there, he continues to lead retreats and teach meditation, while also running the counselling business *Talking Listening Clarity*. www.danapriya.org

ISBN 978 1 911407 59 1
160 pages

First Aid Kit for the Mind
Breaking the Cycle of Habitual Behaviours
Valerie (Vimalasara) Mason-John

Heal from the habits that limit you.

Keep this small book close for those moments when you need inspiration, guidance and the courage to deal with your impulses skilfully.

'*This inspiring and insightful book left me in absolute awe of Mason-John's wisdom and guidance as one of the premier social, cultural and psychological healers of our time.*' – Kenneth V. Hardy

'*This is a user-friendly guide for meeting our minds with kindness and compassion even when we're struggling the most.*' – Sharon Salzberg

'*An entertaining, succinct and highly practical primer to help us get through the many challenging moments life has a way of throwing at us.*' – Gabor Maté, MD

'*This is a lovely and essential book. Lovely in its presentation, in its practical tips and personal stories; essential in looking in a kind and wise way at patterns and triggers.*' – Martine Batchelor

'*This is the most directly practical set of tools for dealing with addiction and underlying trauma I've ever read.*' – Kevin Griffin

Valerie (Vimalasara) Mason-John is the co-author of *Eight Step Recovery: Using the Buddha's Teachings to Overcome Addiction* and co-founder of its related award-winning recovery programme. Vimalasara works as a Compassionate Inquiry therapist and mindfulness practitioner, and a recovery and life coach. They are ordained into the Triratna Buddhist Order.

ISBN 978 1 915342 23 2
176 pages

Sangharakshita
The Boy, the Monk, the Man
Nagabodhi

A monk, a man, a writer and a poet; founder of the Triratna Buddhist Order and Community – a pioneering worldwide Buddhist movement. An audacious reformer, and for some a deeply controversial figure. In an absorbing narrative, Nagabodhi takes us on a journey through the twists and turns of Sangharakshita's life; the experiences, insights and reflections that nurtured his approach as a teacher; and the legacy he left behind.

'...*a wonderfully engaging account of the life and work of a remarkable man*....' – Maitreyabandhu, author of *Life with Full Attention* and founder of PoetryEast

'*He led the way in the West in creating a viable model of how a non-monastic sangha community could work – as well as among the Dalits in India. ...a tremendous achievement requiring great vision, self-sacrifice and determination, not to mention hard work, courage, patience and perhaps one might say a certain degree of audacity*....' – Lama Shenpen Hookham, founder of the Awakened Heart Sangha and author of *The Buddha Within* and other titles

'*Consistently subtle, perceptive and engaging, this book is a vivid description of what it was like to be around Sangharakshita and a perceptive account of Sangharakshita's growing understanding of what it means to live an authentic Buddhist life*....' – Vishvapani Blomfield, author of *Gautama Buddha: The Life and Teachings of the Awakened One*

Nagabodhi joined Sangharakshita's new Buddhist Order in 1974 and has given his life to a range of Triratna projects in the UK and abroad. He worked closely with Sangharakshita, sometimes living in communities with him. In 1982 they travelled on tour in India, an adventure Nagabodhi chronicled in *Jai Bhim! Dispatches from a Peaceful Revolution*.

ISBN 978-1-911407-97-3
384 pages